# Black Love Matters

# Black Love Matters

## Authentic Men's Voices on Marriages and Romantic Relationships

Armon R. Perry

LEXINGTON BOOKS
*Lanham • Boulder • New York • London*

Published by Lexington Books
An imprint of The Rowman & Littlefield Publishing Group, Inc.
4501 Forbes Boulevard, Suite 200, Lanham, Maryland 20706
www.rowman.com

6 Tinworth Street, London SE11 5AL, United Kingdom

British Library Cataloguing in Publication Information Available

**Library of Congress Cataloging-in-Publication Data**

Library of Congress Control Number: 2020942745

ISBN 978-1-7936-2204-4 (cloth)
ISBN 978-1-7936-2206-8 (pbk)
ISBN 978-1-7936-2205-1 (electronic)

This book is dedicated to the
courageous and insightful brothas
who took the time to share their stories with me
to make this project possible.

# Contents

# Introduction

I have always been interested in topics concerning black people and black families in particular. As a black man, I literally have skin in the game. Beyond self-interest, my upbringing certainly played a significant role in my motivation for studying black families and the factors that influence them. As a son of the deep south, race has also always been front and center. As a teenager, I did not need a PhD to understand that my people were treated differently than white people and that the disparate treatment had direct and meaningful implications on the ways in which families functioned including male-female relationships, socialization around courtship and dating, as well as union formation. All I needed was to be bused from my socially, politically, and economically disadvantaged neighborhood to an (at the time) affluent high school named in honor of the first president of the Confederacy to see how structural inequality and discrimination contributed to creating the types of psychological stress and economic strain that prevented union formation in some cases and devastated established or developing relationships in others. You see, it was at Jefferson Davis Sr. High School that for the first time I could clearly distinguish the haves from the have nots. Every single day I left a neighborhood where having a car with power windows and working air conditioning was the benchmark for success to sit in class with teenagers who drove BMW 325is. Every single day I watched my grandmother go to work in the housekeeping department at a local hospital while making friends with kids who had their rooms cleaned for them by the family housekeeper. Every single day, I watched people in my neighborhood surveilled, harassed, and accosted by the police while my friends from school engaged in just as much, if not more deviant and sometimes illegal behavior only to walk away unscathed because their parents were friends or close associates of the police. So, it was against this backdrop that I first began to take an interest in examining family life and how it was shaped by environmental factors. After seeing the juxtapositions between what I saw in my neighborhood and what I saw at school, I could not unsee them. Therefore, I would engage people in discussions about the form, function, and roles of relationships and family every chance I got. However, the most impactful discussions and experiences I had were the Friday afternoon sessions with the older guys from the neighborhood whose *mentoring* focused exclusively on pressuring us to chase girls, get their phone numbers, and eventually add them to our list of *beats* (i.e., name given to a girl we would potentially have sex with). In this ritual of counting our beats, we would call the unsuspecting female on 3-way and engage them in a discussion that would eventually take on a sexual nature, ultimately resulting in a proposition. A positive response from the girl would serve as confirmation that we were indeed, *the man*. Despite my contempt for these calls which were clear violations of trust, I could never muster up the gumption to outwardly or verbally object. Therefore, I regularly caved under the peer pressure to avoid the relentless ridicule that awaited anyone who could not respond in the affirmative to the question, "Say homeboy, where ya beats at?" Needless to say, these experiences colored the way I saw romantic relationships between black men and women. They taught me that relationships were less about commitment, honesty, and shared interests and more about gamesmanship, leverage, and manipulation. In the process, I adopted a play or get played mindset. As a result, I was reluctant to trust others and certainly would not open up or be vulnerable with them. Put another way, I was always on guard—it was as if I was going through my relationships or interactions with the opposite sex like the world was listening on the other end of one of those 3-way phone calls. Since my teenage years, although I matured beyond being influenced by what I thought my homeboys thought, the effects of these early experiences remained as many of my girlfriends would complain that I was aloof and would describe me as distant and not fully engaged. Even my wife, to whom I've been married for over a decade often laments that I am "selfish with my feelings." Despite my emotional selfishness, I am not looking to hide anything. However, it is certainly true that I rarely talk about how I feel and would much rather discuss what I think.

Over the years, I learned that my so-called selfishness with my feelings was not all that uncommon among men, especially black men. In fact, in my experience, being reserved in this manner was more rule than exception. This was, of course, the case until about 10 years ago when things started to change with the release of Steve Harvey's, *Act Like a Lady, Think Like a Man*. When this book came out, it was as if the sky opened up and the Da Vinci Code had been cracked. Large numbers of people in my circle of influence were reading and talking about this book. Folks were discussing it everywhere. And when I say everywhere, I mean everywhere. At school, they were reading it. At work, they were reading it. In the barber shops and beauty salons, they were reading it. I even overheard a few discussions about it at the Smoothie King that I frequented after working out at the gym.

Given my lifelong interest in black families, I loved that people were talking about black male-female romantic relationships. This was so much the case that I even picked up a copy for myself. However, upon reading it, I found the book to be a chronicling of Steve Harvey's individual thoughts and perspectives on romantic relationships. This was quite different than the way I perceived that people, at least those that I came into contact with, were receiving it. In my experience, people were touting the book as if it were a how-to guide for finding and keeping a *good* black man rather than as a behind the scenes look into Steve Harvey's personal take on romantic relationships. Coming to this realization, my initial excitement turned into confusion and dismay. To be specific, I could not figure out why the people around me received the book the way that they did because neither was it grounded in relationship research nor did it feature the narratives or lived experiences of anyone other than Steve Harvey himself. To be clear, this is not to criticize Steve Harvey or anyone else for that matter. Certainly, he is more than entitled to his perspective and even documenting that perspective in the form of a book. However, by all accounts, Steve Harvey is not a relationship expert professionally trained to offer relationship advice or best practices. Moreover, his celebrity status leads me to believe that the nature and dynamics of his romantic relationships are significantly different from those of the vast majority of his readers. Harvey's fame, wealth, and the associated world view would likely create a disconnect between the game plan he spelled out in his book and the experiences shaping it vis-à-vis those of most of his readers. I wondered how many black women walked away feeling disheartened after signing up to read the men's "playbook," only to find out that they had only been given access to the world according to Steve Harvey. Nevertheless, one thing was for sure—the interest generated by *Act Like Lady* made it clear that there was a demand for discourse on black men's perspectives on romantic relationships.

As a result of this demand, I became more intrigued than ever by what I saw as a burgeoning academic field and a popular culture cottage industry focused on finding and keeping a good black man. Therefore, in response, I set out to bring some balance to the literature. In order to do so, I collected stories from a group of diverse and authentic black men, a group that is often discussed, but rarely, if ever featured in firsthand accounts about their own lived experiences. In all, I interviewed thirty-three men and followed them over the course of four years, tracking the changes in their relationship attitudes, trajectories, and statuses. Given the long history of black men being implicated and deficit framed in public and academic discourses related to the family, *Black Love Matters* represents one of very few collections of black men from across the age, educational, and socioeconomic spectrums speaking for themselves about their romantic relationships and the experiences shaping them. It is in this void, at the intersection of popular culture and qualitative research, where *Black Love Matters* is situated. However, to be clear, *Black Love Matters* is not a dating or relationship book. It is not intended to serve as a how-to guide for singles looking to hook up or attract a partner. Nor is it designed as a healthy marriage or relationship education reference guide or curriculum. Rather, *Black Love Matters* is simply an attempt to give voice to adult black men who are often discussed and targeted in pop culture and public policy but are rarely empowered to share their stories. As such, *Black Love Matters* centers on the men sharing their authentic narratives. In sharing their narratives, the participants exhibit a range of masculinities and representations of blackness. In so doing, the themes that emerge in *Black Love Matters* include familiar tropes such as gender roles, sex and infidelity, family structure and economics, as well as newer and more fertile ground like relationship trajectories, the impact of trauma, and role of romantic relationships in identity formation.

As *Black Love Matters* unfolds, its layout includes seven chapters covering myriad aspects of the men's lives and lived experiences. Chapter 1, "From *Act Like a Lady, Think Like a Man* to *4:44*," lays the foundation for the men's narratives. It provides an overview of significant media representations and academic literature on black men's views on marriage and romantic relationships in popular culture in the ten years between the release of Steve Harvey's aforementioned book and hip-hop icon, Jay-Z's most recent solo album in which the often distant, detached, and cocky emcee opens up about his infidelity, the lessons he learned from the pain it caused both him and his family, and his efforts to repair his marriage. This chapter is co-authored with Dr. Siobhan Smith, a communications professor whose expertise is in the area of media studies. Together, Dr. Smith and I examine the recent media and research on black men and their roles in romantic relationships. In doing so, we make the case that we are currently in a golden age of black masculinity in which there are now more representations or allowances for diverse portrayals or openness/receptivity to black men being vulnerable and discussing their emotions than ever before.

Chapter 2, "Setting the Stage," serves to introduce readers to the study's methods and setting. The chapter offers insight into some of the predominant overarching themes, while also providing a brief profile of each of the study participants. These profiles, designed to supply a more intimate look at the men, include relevant demographic data and relationship status, as well as the men's responses to questions about their ideal mates and a marriage perceptions word association ice breaker. This chapter also offers a closer look at the study's setting, Louisville, Kentucky. As the largest city in the northernmost southern state, Louisville or *Possibility City*, as it is called by the Chamber of

Commerce offers an interesting backdrop for an examination of black men's romantic relationships for a number of reasons. In fact, I've often referred to Louisville as a place that Goldilocks would like because of its *just right* feel. It's not too big, but it's not too small. It's not the deep south, but it's not the northeast or midwest. Louisville also features a unique juxtaposition of a thriving black middle class while also having the dubious distinction of being named one of the most segregated cities in the country. Thus, for these and other reasons that are detailed in the chapter, Louisville provides an ideal canvass for an exploration of black men's perspectives and experiences in marriage and romantic relationships.

Chapter 3, "Let's Talk about Sex," covers the men's sexual attitudes, behaviors, and the role that sex plays in shaping their romantic relationships. In it, the men share their thoughts on topics ranging from their receptivity to engaging in casual sex to discussions about the men's interest in achieving intimacy with their partners. This chapter was written with Dr. Cheri Langley, a public health scholar whose research experience includes work in the areas of adolescent sexual behavior and factors predicting sexual debut.

Chapter 4, "Trials, Tribulations & Trauma," is an examination of the men's experiences with various forms of trauma, a topic that has received scant attention in the literature. Included in these discussions are the men's experience and exposure to psychological trauma, physical trauma, and relationship trauma and the ways in which they impact the men's past, present, and future romantic relationships. This chapter is co-authored with Dr. Azaliah Israel, an emerging scholar whose work has shined a light on issues impacting black fathers and masculinity.

Chapter 5, "A Change Gonna Come," chronicles the men's relationship trajectories over time. To do so, I highlight the type and number of the men's relationship transitions over the 4-year study period. The chapter also presents contextual information about the experiences contributing to or shaping those transitions.

Chapter 6, "Love and Manhood," addresses identity development. Specifically, in this chapter, the men discuss the extent to which being involved in a relationship is salient to their identity as a man. In sharing their perspectives, the men touch on concepts including but not limited to gender roles, economics, and fatherhood as identity defining.

Chapter 7, "Recaps and Reflections," is dedicated to summarizing the book's major findings and the men discussing the advice they would give to anyone with an interest in what black men think about romantic relationships and marriages. Based on the major findings and the men's advice, the chapter wraps up with some recommendations for professionals whose work interfaces with black men and their romantic partners.

## Chapter One

# From *Act Like a Lady, Think Like a Man* to 4:44

## with Dr. Siobhan Smith

### BLACK MEN, MARRIAGE, AND
### ROMANTIC RELATIONSHIPS IN THE MEDIA

Currently, we are witnessing an increase of black male-focused works in the media. This period began about a decade ago. These works either center on the black male experience or feature black male characters that have impactful narratives. Of particular interest is the salient role that romantic relationships play in the in the lives of the black men in these media. It would not be overstating to argue that we are witnessing a Golden Age of Revelatory Black Male Media. Contextualizing this current era in televised fictional narratives and referring to HBO's *Treme*, Jones (2016) argues that these current offerings are challenging mainstream trends. He states:

> Understanding the Third Golden Age of television in this context allows me to frame *Treme*—a canonical series of the art form—in blackness, which complements the cable television drama's penchant for alternative narratives that engage serious themes related to race, sex, gender, and class.

At the movies, romantic comedies including *Why Did I Get Married Too?* (2010, directed by Tyler Perry), *The Best Man Holiday* (2013, directed by Malcolm D. Lee), and *About Last Night* (2014; directed by Steve Pink), brought an African American sensibility to the genre. Perry and Lee's sequels illustrated the desire for audiences to see more of the lives of some of their favorite characters. Obie Henderson (2013) states:

> Malcolm D. Lee is a fascinating, underrated filmmaker. Even in his less successful features, he's fascinated with the notion of masculinity, specifically

black masculinity, a topic that runs through his entire canon . . . Lee continues this examination with "The Best Man Holiday," retroactively elevating his original with the deeper shadings he brings to his characters here. We feel as if all parties have grown, and there are some tender moments between the gentlemen that shatter the stereotypical warrior tough-guy standards of expectation. (para. 10–11)

Though the film is a romantic comedy, it continues where the last film left off, exploring the psyches of black men, their relationships, and even the nuances of their relationships with each other.

Meanwhile, thrillers such as David M. Rosenthal's *The Perfect Guy* (2015) and *When the Bough Breaks* (2016, directed by Jon Cassar), focused on what happens when the desire for love goes wrong, such as finding a stable partner and a trustworthy surrogate. Denzel Washington's *Fences* (2016) showed that African American film goers also care about black male characters who are relatable in their struggles (e.g., playwright August Wilson's Troy Maxson whose need to provide and protect his family leads to his own demise).

In addition to books and film, more black men appeared on television as well. For example, Courtney A. Kemp's *Power* (2014), Lee Daniels and Danny Strong's *Empire* (2015), *Queen Sugar* (2016; produced by Ama DuVernay, Melissa Carter, and Oprah Winfrey), and *The Chi* (2018; produced by Lena Waithe, Common, Elwood Reid, Aaron Kaplan, and Rick Famuyiwa) illustrate how past decisions and situations continue to influence the present of black men. For instance, in *Power*, James "Ghost" St. Patrick wants nothing more than to leave his crime-ridden past behind him, but cannot. Ghost also finds himself at the center of a love triangle with his wife and his former girlfriend. Though this is admittedly a recurrent theme in black media, the show does possess, according to Jazmin Kopotsha of Grazia, "really fucking dedicated audience members" (2017, para. 1). She writes:

Season one kicks off on the opening night of Ghost and Tommy's club TRUTH, but as the series progresses, we find out that Ghost kind of wants to straighten up, leave the drug world behind and move forward in life as a club owner. Tommy ain't happy about it. Neither is his wife, Tasha. Beyond that, there's so much more drama and tension of course. And lots of sex. And drugs. And parallel storylines that are actually interesting to follow. Honest. (para. 5)

The books, films, and television shows we mentioned above are *not* meant to be an exhaustive list. Though these descriptions are brief, the range of media provide evidence that the powers that be recognize the importance of providing credible representations of black men's lives (at least from the perspective of their profits). However, all of these works illustrate the complexities of black men's lives, especially with regard to identity and marriage/

romantic relationships. With the brief reviews of these media as a backdrop, next we focus on four specific media texts that we feel are particularly illustrative of *Black Love Matters* and the priority it places on highlighting the range of contemporary black men's narratives.

To start, Steve Harvey's *Act Like a Lady, Think Like a Man: What Men Really Think About Love, Relationships, Intimacy, and Commitment* (2009) is a "playbook" (p. 5) for women to

> Get into a man's mind-set and understand him better, so that you can put into play your plans, your dreams, and your desires, and best of all, you can figure out if he's planning to be with you or just playing with you. (p. 7)

Harvey provides the assumed female reader with "types" of black men (e.g., "Mama's boys"), as well as rules (e.g., the "90 Day Probation[ary period]): if many employers wait 90 days before an employee is "in," then women should wait the same amount of time before engaging in sexual relationships with potential romantic partners. Some media sources, such as ABC News (2009), supported Harvey's relationship book, referring to it as a "great [read] (para. 3)" and stating that "a woman could learn a lot if she would "Act Like a Lady, Think Like a Man."" (para. 2). As a result of the book's popularity, it became a romantic comedy, though the source material is a self-help book. In fairness, this is quite similar to the treatment self-help book *He's Just Not That into You* (2004) received—it also became a romantic comedy in 2009.

However, Jeff Carroll (2011) of *Real Health* states that Harvey's advice does not apply to all, or even most, men. Nico Lang of the *Huffington Post* offers a stronger critique, arguing that the book and the film are "crazy sexist" (para. 1). He writes:

> Through his work, Harvey seems to think that he's empowering women into respecting themselves, but all the book and the film do is teach women that they need to lie, cheat, manipulate, beg, borrow and steal to get into a relationship. Although Harvey loves and respects women, he doesn't value their power enough to allow them to be their own women. . . . The message here is that women can be strong and empowered, only as long as their power or success still caters to male power and ego. As the opening credits tell us: "It's a man's world." (2012, para. 2)

By contrast to Harvey's book, Tarell Alvin McCraney's *Moonlight* (2016) was originally a semi-autobiographical play before it appeared on the silver screen. McCraney wrote this work, *In Moonlight Black Boys Look Blue*, in the Summer of 2003. *Moonlight* is the result of McCraney and director Barry Jenkins' collaboration over several years (Rodriguez 2016). This film tells the story of Chiron in three phases of his life: as "Little," "Chiron," and then as "Black." Of particular focus is his troubled relationships with his drug-addicted mother, his childhood friend/lover, school-yard bullies, and Juan, a drug dealer who acts as a father-figure to him. It is also one of the first films to openly explore black queer masculinity. Randolph (2017) writes, "If you are a queer black man, then the sensation [of seeing oneself on the screen] is arresting and reflective, and no film in recent memory has captured the black queer imagination the way that *Moonlight* has" (p. 383). Critical and popular audiences alike appreciated *Moonlight*, as it received Best Picture honors from both the Golden Globes and the Academy Awards.

Ultimately, *Moonlight* is a testament that regardless of sexual identities, the experience of being a black male in America is an enduring one: "although Jenkins is straight, "Moonlight" is also his story. While reshaping McCraney's original material, he drew on his own life for inspiration" (Rodriguez 2016). In fact, by "queering" black masculinities, Jordan and Brooms (2017) posit that *Moonlight* reflects a range of black masculinities that media rarely explore. In one of the most intimate scenes in the film, Juan teaches Little how to swim. According to Jordan and Brooms (2017):

> Juan gently places Chiron's head in the water and tells him to relax and that he will not let him go . . . this scene allows Chiron to explore his own identity; Chiron can fully be, and explore, himself around Juan where he could not be around other black boys. (p. 144).

Another scene in the movie, during the "Chiron" portion, shows him and his only enduring friend, Kevin, talking on the beach, under the light of the moon. Their unmasking of their innermost selves is punctuated with them kissing. In this scene:

> Kevin and Chiron were not hardened men putting up a tough guise to avoid being seen as "soft" . . . Chiron is gay, Kevin is bisexual. Chiron apologizes for the sexual encounter, but Kevin reassures him that he had nothing to be sorry for, echoing, indirectly, Juan's message about being oneself and being okay with that choice. (Jordan & Brooms 2017 p. 148)

The current Golden Age of Revelatory Black Male Media would not be complete without the inclusion of queer experiences and identities; however, we need more media representations of black queer men across a range of various media.

In addition to the silver screen, television is also a site for the exploration of black men's lives. Specifically, the *New York Times* describes Donald Glover's *Atlanta* (2016) as "Dry and offbeat, with an immediate, original voice, this comedy is a back-roads drive through the expansive territory between rags and riches" (Poniewozik 2016, para. 3). *Rolling Stone* questions if the show should be considered a crime drama, an absurdist comedy, or a character study of the city of Atlanta (Sheffield 2018). Sheffield describes the show as:

> *Atlanta* is Glover's brainchild—he stars as Earnest "Earn" Marks, a guy who went to Princeton, dropped out, wound up broke and desperate back home in Atlanta. Now he struggles to get over by managing his cousin Alfred, a rapper who goes by the *nom du hip-hop* Paper Boi. . . . Earn can't catch a break whatever he does—the whole world stunts on him, whether he's trying to get a good night's sleep in a storage unit or live large at the strip club. He's got a kid with his off-and-on girlfriend Vanessa . . . but he feels like a failure at both roles. (2018 para. 2).

With *Atlanta*, Glover tackles many issues that impact the black experience and particularly those of black males, including but not limited to family dynamics, the desire to be successful in one's chosen field, the tense relationship between blacks and the police, crime in one's community, and cultural (mis)appropriation. Because of Glover's fearless desire to tackle these tensions and more, Sheffield refers to the show as the "best on TV" (para. 1).

While black artists are exploring their lives through the film and television mediums, music is also a fruitful venue for black expression. Though hip-hop fans first knew Jay-Z as a former-drug-dealer-turned-music-mogul, each of his albums have stripped away his rap persona to reveal the black man underneath. His latest release, *4:44* (2017) is arguably his most intimate offering. According to the rapper himself, he woke up at 4:44AM to record tracks for the album. As 4s figure prominently in Jay-Z's and Beyonce's relationship, he directly responds to the confessional nature of her album, *Lemonade*. In these lyrics, Jay-Z admits to his failures as an unfaithful husband and repents his wrongdoings. For instance, he states his horror at "almost going Eric Benet," that is, losing his wife and children to another man. Reeves (2017) writes for *Rolling Stone*:

> If you know anything about Jay-Z's illustrious and groundbreaking career as a rapper, label owner, entrepreneur and "business, man," it's that the Brooklyn native rarely has had time for apologies. . . . So it's unnerving to hear him apologize to his wife, Beyoncé Knowles, on the title track to his 13th album, *4:44.* (para 1–2)

In our opinion, Jay-Z's confessional openness is surprising because men, particularly black men, have constructed their lives around the "cool pose;" and this construction has been reinforced through mediated portrayals, including rap music. This genre is not receptive to sensitivity, nor vulnerability from black men. Pinn (1996) explains that "The sense of manhood exemplified in [rap] music, while allowing for survival, results in the manipulation and harm of black people because of its reliance upon aggression, dominance, and control as the hallmarks of masculine identity" (p. 28).

On *4:44*, Jay-Z also acknowledges his own vulnerabilities as a result of not having a father in his life and accepts his mother as a lesbian. *Variety*'s Andrew Barker (2017) echoes *Rolling Stone*'s sentiments:

> "You got a daughter, gotta get softer," [Jay-Z] tells himself as the album opens, and for him, softness might just be the final frontier. There's still no real gold-standard model for chasing relevance as a middle-aged rapper, but by finally opting out of the race, Jay-Z could well have drawn up a new blueprint.

Jay-Z's "softening" of himself, that is, putting an end to his stage persona, reflects evidence of the Golden Age of Revelatory Black Male Media; however, the artist's success in revealing his true(r) self is also encouraged by this era.

The take-away from all of these works is that black men do not easily negotiate their romantic relationships, as they deal with internal struggles that impact said romantic relationships. In fact, black women, who obviously have the majority of interactions with black men, are desperate for insight and understanding of the men they love. So much so, that when comedian/television personality Steve Harvey offered a solution, *Act Like a Lady, Think Like a Man* it sold two million copies, prompting an updated and expanded edition of the book (2014). Halford (2009) lamented on the release of the first edition of the book:

> Oh, single ladies, single ladies. Are things so very bad that more than a million of you have turned to Steve "The Steve Harvey Show" Harvey for advice on how to catch a man? That's a rhetorical question: of course things are bad, and of course there will always be demand for books acknowledging that men "are simple," that from birth they are forced to confront a looming manhood, and that even when they grow up "the pursuit of manhood" remains their primary objective. (para. 1)

Given the findings from recent research indicating that many black men reflect on popular culture and media to inform and define their ideas about being a man and masculine identity (Goodwill et al. 2019; Malton 2010) *Black Love Matters*, which focuses squarely on the lived experiences of black men, is situated between both popular culture and academic scholarship. This book is able to relate to popular media texts, but also has relevance for rigorous scholarship that focuses on black men. As such, it is important to understand the academic research that has been published during the same ten-year period between *Act Like a Lady* and *4:44*.

## Research on Black Men in Marriage and Romantic Relationships

Much like the research from previous eras, most of the academic research on black marriages and romantic relationships published between *Act Like a Lady* and *4:44* paints a bleak picture. To be specific, this research indicates that marriage rates for blacks have declined significantly since the 1960s and 1970s when over 60 percent of black adults were married, compared to only approximately 30 percent of contemporary blacks being married (Blackman et al. 2005; Cohen and Pepin 2018). Moreover, black people who do marry are more likely than their white counterparts to divorce and are less likely to remarry after divorce (Dixon 2014). Black men and women report lower expectations of marriage than other groups, and black women regularly report lower levels of marriage and relationship satisfaction than white men and women, as well as black men (Lincoln, Taylor, and Jackson 2008). The most frequently posited explanations are related to economics and their role in union formation. In other words, for decades, researchers have argued that black men have been locked out of traditional avenues for securing financial resources due to discrimination. As a result of this disadvantaged financial status, many of them are not able to fulfill their socially prescribed roles as providers and breadwinners. As such, they are viewed as less desirable marriage mates by black women, who like women of other races, often seek to marry up by partnering with a man who is educationally and economically superior (Dixon 2014). As a result, large numbers of black women opt to wait longer than others to marry or forgo the institution altogether. Researchers have also weighed in on the ways in which black men's financial challenges affect their attitudes toward marriage. According to Bethea and Allen (2013), men who cannot live up to their partner's or society's economic expectations oftentimes react by withdrawing emotionally or physically from their relationship. This can also sometimes contribute to men feeling worthless. In response, many become defensive or emotionally guarded until they attempt to exercise control over their relationship by seeking out sexual relationships with other women (Benjamin 2014). Allen and Helm (2013) also discuss the role of egalitarianism as a threat to intimacy among disadvantaged black men and women. The authors explain that although egalitarianism may be viewed as a strength of many black male-female couples, this is only the case when both parties find shared power and decision making desirable. They go on to explain that in some instances, black men may seek to establish a dominant position in their relationships as a compensatory mechanism for their financial shortcomings. When this happens, women's financial independence may lead to men's frustration as some men may fear that they will be mocked for their tenuous financial standing or worse, the woman may leave them if they experience an economic loss.

So pervasive in the literature on black marriages and romantic relationships are these economic explanations and their consequences that they have led to the development of theoretical frameworks for describing discord in black male-female relationships. For example, Franklin and Pillow (2014) offered the Prince Charming Ideal. In this model, mature and responsible manhood is grounded in the philosophical belief that men are to assume a protective, providing, and patriarchal role regarding their female mate. According to the framers, the ideal took on more relevance to black men and women in a post Civil Rights Era wherein black men with the requisite education and income had more opportunities to assert themselves as men in ways that approximated white men. This ideal is both learned and reinforced through formal and informal socialization processes in educational and religious institutions, as well as through the mass media. Black men who both internalize the Prince Charming Ideal and have the resources to act in accordance with it are rewarded in that they generally experience positive interactions with their female partners. However, for black men who either reject the Prince Charming Ideal or internalize it, but cannot act in accordance with it, their relationships are fraught with obstacles and challenges as these men are likely to respond to the real or perceived pressure to conform by becoming hyper critical of the female, making extreme demands on her in order to provide himself with an excuse to not fulfill his role. In other, more dangerous cases, internalizing the ideal and not having the resources associated with its manifestation can contribute to the black man having low self-esteem and feeling as if he is not respected by his female partner, leading him to become aggressive, domineering, and even potentially abusive.

Clearly, the extant research has shed light on the role that racism has played in black male-female relationship troubles by restricting black men's opportunities and ability to secure and maintain gainful employment or income sufficient to provide for a wife and family. However, some of the research published in the last 10 years offers an alternate perspective on the ways in which racism and discrimination negatively impact black male-female romantic relationships and marriages.

Simons et al. (2012) tested the proposition that youth exposure to race related disadvantages and stressors like discrimination, poverty, crime, and harsh parenting would contribute to distrusting relational schemas that would increase the probability of negative romantic relationships in late adolescence and early adulthood. The authors analyzed data from a sample of 337 African Americans participating in a multi-site study of neighborhood and family effects on health and development. Data analysis revealed that persistent exposure to discrimination, crime, and financial strain were associated with a cynical and distrustful view of people and relationships. This was particularly true for African American males, leading to the conclusion that African American males encounter high levels and more serious forms of discrimination result- ing in more dramatic and negative impacts on their relational schemas than African American females. Similarly, Kogan, Yu, and Brown (2016) studied romantic relationship commitment among emerging adult African American men. Their analysis found that racial discrimination exacerbated the impact of harsh, unsupportive parenting because it meant that there was no protection available from deleterious environmental factors, thus the men learned to not trust others in the context of their relationships.

Jewell (2014) examined black male-female conflict through the lens of imagery and internalized perceptions. Here, the author argued that black men and women are repeatedly exposed to stereotyped, negative, and distorted images of one another in both academic and pop culture spaces. The effect of this constant exposure is the creation of nonconstructive and negative perceptions of the opposite sex such as the finding that many black women do not feel that black men assume responsibility for functions tra- ditionally assigned to men and that they believe that black men expect too much support and assistance from black women in their efforts to become socially and economically successful. In sum, the author concluded that many black men and women adopt negative perceptions assigned to them which creates a foundation for mistrust and skepticism from the outset of their relationships.

In addition to the deleterious effects of poverty, racism, and discrimina- tion, it is also the case that even more advantaged blacks have experienced disproportionately high declines in marriage rates. In *Is Marriage for White People?: How African American Marriage Decline Affects Everyone,* Banks (2012) states that although research, public policy, and social commentary has focused on marriage among low income blacks, there also exists a mar- riage gap among middle income blacks as the highest earning black men are more than twice as likely as their white counterparts to never marry. To explain the marriage gap among middle class blacks, Banks (2012) pointed to the gender imbalance in which black women have too few available black men of similar financial status to choose from for marriage. The result of this imbalance has been that concurrent sexual relationships or "man-sharing" is more common among blacks than other groups which makes sustaining com- mitted intimate relationships difficult because the surplus of black women makes remaining single enticing. Banks continued that successful black men are highly sought-after, very picky, and can develop and maintain unrealisti- cally high standards because of the variety of women that they have enjoyed.

Similarly, May's (2001) *Talking at Trena's: Everyday Conversations at an African American Tavern* is an ethnographic account of middle-income black men's experiences and discussions at a local tavern. The book revealed that the men's relationships were often confronted with challenges and threats grounded in tensions in black male-female relationships. The author concluded that although the men viewed marriage and even shackin' (non-marital cohabitating) as an honorable sign that a man was maturing and taking care of his responsibilities, they recognized infidelity as acceptable for men, but not women. In fact, the men had clear expectations that in order for marriage to work, women needed to have sex regularly, take care of the children, and contribute financially. So engrained were these stereotypes and double standards that the men reacted suspiciously to women who they felt wanted expensive things too early in a relationship. As such, some of the men would ridicule others and label them as hen-pecked if they spent large amounts of time or money with new girlfriends. Finally, the men responded adversely to girlfriends and wives who were too demanding or suffocating. In these cases, the discussion in the tavern revolved around developing strategies to divorce or get out of a bad situation with little conflict, losing contact with children, or suffering any financial/material penalty. In sum, the discussions and behaviors of many of the men in the tavern served to create or reaffirm the type of distrust between black men and women that prevents new relationships and threatens existing relationships, possibly contributing to the declines in black marriage rates.

A review of the literature also reveals other threats to black male-female romantic relationships and marriages, regardless of income. These include the extended family and the increased use of technology, both of which can produce distrust. As it relates to the extended family, it has most often been characterized as a strength of black families. However, in some cases, either or both members of a couple are so inextricably linked to and dependent upon their extended family that their commitment to the kin network threatens the strength of the relationship or marriage (Dixon 2014). With regard to technology and its role in declining marriage rates, the increased use of social networking has become ubiquitous in contemporary society (Bergdall et al. 2012). As Allen and Helm (2013) point out, on one hand, this technology provides pathways for connecting and maintaining relationships. However, widespread access to technology has also created more opportunities to violate trust through communicating with former partners, engaging in internet affairs or pornography, or offering couples avenues for getting their emotional needs met outside of their relationship. As *Black Love Matters* unfolds, the men's stories corroborate the pro and con nature of both the extended family and increased use of technology and the ways that they can either serve to support or harm romantic relationships and marriages.

## Lifting Up Black Men's Voices

One of the major weaknesses of the existing literature is that despite the amount of attention paid to black men's roles in the dissolution of romantic relationships and marriages, there are very few studies of black male-female relationships that feature the firsthand perspectives of black men. However, a series of studies conducted by Dr. Tera Hurt has given voice to the narratives of black men. These studies were published between 2012–2017 and feature data collected from 52 married black men who were participating in a healthy marriage intervention. In the first of these studies, Hurt (2012) examined the meanings that black men ascribed to marriage. Qualitative data analysis revealed that the emergent themes revolved around the men's interests in seeking emotional support, lifelong commitment, enhanced life success, and secure attachments as their reasons for viewing marriage favorably. Subsequently, Hurt (2014) interviewed 52 married black men inquiring into their thought processes and the factors influencing the decision to marry. When the men discussed the factors that encouraged them to marry, they invoked their wife's characteristics, their spirituality, a deep desire to be together with their wives, as well as feeling encouraged from others in their circles of influence. With regard to their perspectives on the barriers to marriage, the men cited that marriage represented a perceived loss of freedom, financial barriers, previous negative relationship experiences, and disapproval from friends and family. That same year, Hurt et al. (2014) engaged black men in discussions focused on explaining why they thought black women were disproportionately single. The sample included 52 married black men participating in a healthy marriage intervention study who were largely middle class, religious, and had been with their partners an average of 16 years. The findings revealed that some of the men felt that women's independence and self-reliant attitudes may be undermining union formation and long-term commitments. It was also the case that a significant proportion of the study participants discussed the need for marriage education and socialization. Moreover, these same participants referenced the lack of marriage education programs and the difficulty that black men and women have in reaching individual milestones like educational achievement and gainful employment are also contributing factors to the relatively low rates of marriage among black women. Most recently, Hurt et al. (2017) explored married black men's observations of their fathers' teachings about husbandhood. In this qualitative analysis, 24 of the 52 married black men interviewed reported having positive marriage role models and 12 reported having negative role models. For those reporting positive role models, their observations centered on themes related to commitment, conflict resolution, fulfilling the roles of protector and provider, showing love and affection, and displaying teamwork and partnership.

Beyond the specific areas where the men reported receiving role modeling, the other major finding was that the men found role models in their biological fathers, as well as other male relatives and social fathers.

This collection of studies makes a very important contribution to the literature. This is because these studies feature black men's perspectives on marriage when very few studies have included them in their samples. Knowing more about what black men think and feel about marriage means that researchers' studies and interventions can be more closely grounded in the lived experiences of those who are most directly impacted. Additionally, as we learned from both the men in Trena's tavern (May 2001) and the Hurt et al. (2017) study on men's observations of the fathers' marital attitudes and behavior, these men will become teachers, socializers, and mentors themselves whose attitudes, philosophies, and behaviors will have implications for the next generation.

Despite the important contributions of previous research on black male-female relationships and marriages, these studies feature samples that are either exclusively young and low income or older married black men who are mostly middle class and religious. Thus, there remains a dearth of literature representing myriad black male relationship attitudes and behaviors. In filling this gap, *Black Love Matters* features men who are varied and diverse with regard to age, educational attainment, socioeconomic status, marital status, and religiosity. Beyond simply filling the gaps in the literature on black marriages and male-female romantic relationships, *Black Love Matters* advances our knowledge as it features exploration into black men's early and contemporary relationship experiences and the contexts shaping them which we know is an important socializing factor in the establishment and maintenance of relationship health (Kogan et al. 2013). Furthermore, *Black Love Matters* features longitudinal data collection, which allows for the changes in the men's relationship trajectories to be considered as a part of its analysis and conclusions. Most importantly, *Black Love Matters* rejects the notion that black men are simple but are indeed complex at their infinite intersections. Moreover, *Black Love Matters* provides an authentic understanding of black manhood and an inside look into the lives of black men as readers will discover the participants' thoughts about their relationships, from their own mouths, in their own voices. Since we hope for black men's lives to be explored more fully in the media and academic research, we offer *Black Love Matters*, which provides the real insights of real black men to provide a deeper understanding for those seeking to become better informed about black men.

*Chapter Two*

# Setting the Stage

This chapter is about introductions. In other words, chapter 2, "Setting the Stage," serves to introduce the study methods, the city of Louisville, and most importantly, the study participants. To be more specific, with regard to the study methods, included here are descriptions of the study sample, how it was recruited, the questions that were asked of the men, and the codes that emanated from the interviews. As it relates to the study setting, brief historical and contemporary discussions are included that frame Louisville, Kentucky as an ideal backdrop for a study on black men's relationship trajectories. Finally, the chapter ends with brief, individual profiles of each of the study participants designed to provide some important context to better understanding the men's perspectives on marriage and romantic relationships at the start of the study. These profiles include the men's pseudonym, age, number of children, highest level of academic achievement, relationship status, and responses to questions about the first word that came to mind when they thought about marriage and the traits and qualities of their ideal marriage mates.

## STUDY METHODS

The research supporting this book was conducted as part of a larger mixed methods study investigating black men's attitudes toward marriage in which the quantitative methods included a survey questionnaire. A targeted community-based sampling procedure was used to recruit participants (Watters and Biernacki 1989), with the primary criteria being their race, gender, and residence within the Louisville, Kentucky metro area. In an attempt to recruit a diverse cross-section of black, adult males, potential participants were recruited from a local university, social service agencies, barbershops, and

philanthropic organizations. Participants completing the survey were queried about their willingness to participate in follow up qualitative interviews
aimed at providing the participants the opportunity to share more detailed and
nuanced insights into their attitudes and experiences related to marriage and
romantic relationships than could be gleaned from a survey questionnaire.
Men expressing a willingness to participate in the qualitative follow up were
contacted by the first author to schedule the interview. These efforts resulted
in a sample which included 33 adult black males. At the time of the first
data collection wave, on average, the men were 41.00 ($sd = 15.88$) years old,
had 1.96 ($sd = .63$) biological children, and had a reported annual income of
$40,674 ($sd = $10,000.64$). Fifteen (45.45%) of the men held either a high
school diploma or a GED, 13 (39.39%) held a college degree, 1 (3.03%) held
neither a high school diploma, nor a GED, and 4 (12.12%) did not report their
level of educational attainment. At the time of the initial data collection, 14
(42.42%) of the men were married to their first and only wife, 9 (27.27%)
were single and had never married, 7 (21.21%) were single as a result of being divorced, and 3 (9.09%) were divorced and re-married.

All interviews were conducted by the first author, a male professor with
a doctorate degree and several years of experience collecting and analyzing
qualitative research. The interviewer had no pre-existing relationship with the
study participants prior to the initial data collection wave. Therefore, at the
outset of each of the initial interviews, the author thanked the participant and
mentioned that the purpose of the study was to solicit black men's perspectives on romantic relationships and marriages to balance out the dearth of such
first-hand accounts in the literature. The author also disclosed that although
he was married, he had no interest in either endorsing or criticizing marriage.
Rather, his interest was in better understanding the men's perspectives and
how their experiences helped to shape them, as well as creating a platform for
the men to share their stories in their own voices, without regard to whether
they were consistent with his own perspectives and experiences. Both the
author's philosophical neutrality related to the merits or stature of marriage
and the emphasis placed on uplifting the men's perspectives are related to his
disciplinary identification as a social worker and its code of ethics which pre-
scribes maintaining a non-judgmental attitude and empowering marginalized
groups through the promotion of self-determination (NASW 2017). All the
interviews were conducted at times and places of the participants' choosing
including locations such as the participants' homes, offices, local restaurants
and coffee shops, in community centers, and in public parks. Although some
interviews were held in public spaces, there were never any other people
contributing to the discussions outside of the author and the participant. The
interviews followed a semi-structured format featuring questions created *a*

*priori* that were grounded in the research literature on marriage and romantic relationships. On average, the interviews lasted 49 minutes each, were audio recorded to ensure accuracy, and were transcribed verbatim. From there, the transcripts were reviewed to identify essential codes highlighting the participants' lived experiences relative to their attitudes and experiences toward marriage and romantic relationships. Using QSR International's NVIVO8 to organize the codes, an iterative process of refining the codes was undertaken until the salient themes that emerged across the interview transcripts were identified. Given the interest in better understanding the men's experiences with marriage and relationships, a phenomenological approach was employed. The intent behind utilizing a phenomenological approach was to learn more about the meaning that the men ascribed to their experiences and the ways in which their marriages and relationships were shaped by them. Moreover, per Creswell (2007), employing this approach positioned the author to give voice to the participants and their narratives. Given that one of the limits of the extant literature is that much of it deficit frames and implicates black men in discussions about what ails black families without taking the men's perspectives into account, employing a method that emphasizes the salience of the men's lived experiences and how they make meaning of them was a priority. Table 2.1 displays the questions and follow up prompts from the qualitative interview scripts.

**Table 2.1.** *Semi Structured Interview Script*

| Question | Prompt/Follow up |
|---|---|
| When you hear the word marriage, what is the first thing that comes to your mind? | |
| How many of your close male friends are married? | |
| Are you currently married or involved in a romantic relationship? | If so, what about this person sets her apart from all the other women that you have been involved with? |
| If married, how did you know you were ready? | Did you arrive at this place on your own or was it something about the woman that made you ready? |
| How do you feel about the institution of marriage? | How would your friends answer this question? |
| What type of women do you prefer? | What are your preferences with regard to personality and physical appearance? |
| In past or current relationships, what are your expectations for your partner? | How often have your partners met your expectations? |
| In your past or current relationships, what are your expectations for yourself? | How often have you met your own expectations? |

*(continued)*

**Table 2.1.** *(continued)*

| Question | Prompt/Follow up |
|---|---|
| In your past or current relationships, what expectations have your partners had for you? | How often have you met these expectations? |
| In your past or current relationships, what have been your biggest complaints about your past and current partners? | |
| In your past or current relationships, what have been your past or current partners' biggest complaints about you? | |
| Considering the three most significant romantic relationships that you have had, what were the major milestones (positive or negative) of the relationship? | Describe the circumstances surrounding these milestones that you identified. |
| Research and reports suggest that significantly fewer black people are likely to get married than their white counterparts. For those who do marry, black people are more likely to divorce than their white counterparts. Why do you think this is the case? | |
| In your opinion, what could be done by individual men and women, as well as policymakers to increase the rates of marriage among black couples? | |
| Of all your experiences, which have had the biggest influence on your current attitude toward marriage? | |

Over the course of the 4-year study period, each participant was interviewed at least twice, with the exception of one participant who passed away before his second interview. The interviews yielded more than 150 hours of digital audio records and 557 pages of text transcripts. The first author coded all of the interviews individually with additional coding taking place for chapters 3 and 4 by their respective co-authors. In all, the coding produced 59 (35 tree codes, 24 free codes) codes of interest. An exhaustive list of these codes and their descriptions is included in table 2.2. Consistent with the tenets of the phenomenological approach, after the interviews were transcribed and the text were coded for emerging themes, they were subsequently grouped into meaning units that led to an overall description of the participants' conceptualizations of marriage and the significant life events and experiences that shaped those conceptualizations. With regard to interpreting the data, per the guidelines of Creswell (2007) and Corbin and Strauss (2014), the coding process helped to tease out many of the nuances in the participants' concepts of marriage or romantic relationships and the ways in which they were articulated throughout the interviews. Subsequently, the participants' experiences and epiphanies were highlighted along with the contexts in which they occurred to present the patterns, processes, and unique features of their lives.

**Table 2.2.  *Black Love Matters Codes***

| Code | Description | Branches |
|---|---|---|
| Race | Participants discussing the impact of race on romantic relationships and marriage. | –Cultural differences<br>–Interracial dating<br>–Racism |
| Utilizing social media | Participants discussing the use of social media to stay connected and span distance and time. | –Social media<br>–Online dating<br>–It goes down in the DMs |
| Good mate traits (possessed) | Participants discussing positive qualities that their partners possess. | –Attractiveness<br>–Length of time together<br>–Personality<br>–Helpfulness<br>–Teacher<br>–Accountability<br>–Ease of love |
| Good mate traits (aspirational) | Participants discussing positive qualities that participants want in a partner. | |
| Geography | Participants making reference to an area of town, a city, or state that participants used to explain values, beliefs, or behavior. | |
| Participant strengths | Participants discussing positive qualities that they or others have recognized in them. | |
| Turn offs | Participants discussing things about partners (current or past) that they don't like. | |
| Newlyweds | Participants discussing the initial stages of their relationship or marriage. | –Being concern free<br>–Figuring relationships out |
| Flaws/baggage | Participant discussing their own negative qualities or traits. | –Insecurities<br>–Fear of Intimacy |
| Marriage Attitudes | Participants discussing their thoughts about marriage. | –Word association- participants<br>–Meaning of marriage |
| Learning/growing together | Participants discussing how their relationship has evolved over time. | |

*(continued)*

Table 2.2.   *(continued)*

| Code | Description | Branches |
|------|-------------|----------|
| Social Capital | Participants discussing how their connections and human resources have been helpful in relationships. | |
| Family matters | Participants discussing their families of origin or extended family. | –Influence of family<br>–Lessons learned from family<br>–Bringing family along<br>–Working with family<br>–Differences in family values<br>–Fictive kin<br>–Extended family<br>–Blended family<br>–In laws |
| Maturing | Participants discussing their individual maturation. | –Coming of age<br>–Boy vs man (internal conflict)<br>–Self reflection<br>–Self awareness |
| Settling down | Participants discussing embracing the idea of marriage. | |
| Timing | Participants discussing how serendipity and random timing impacted relationships. | |
| Relationship transition | Participants discussing the number or circumstances surrounding a change in relationship status. | –Breaking up<br>–Making up<br>–First impression<br>–Take it to the next level |
| Friends/marrying best friend | Participants discussing if/how partner was or is also a friend. | |
| Benefits of marriage or relationships | Participants discussing how they have benefitted from being married. | –Marriage changed me for the better<br>–Marriage partner made me better<br>–Marriage = team<br>–Marriage structures/ organizes life |
| Marriage as a loss | Participants discussing how marriage forced them to give up things they enjoyed while single. | –Things you are presumed to have to give up<br>–Discouraging marriage<br>–Loss of freedom |
| Priorities | Participants discussing their priorities or alluding to the way they prioritize their lives. | |

| Code | Description | Branches |
|------|-------------|----------|
| Things that hurt relationships | Participants discussing attitudes, behaviors, or factors that negatively impact relationships. | −Conflict<br>−Guarded with emotions/ holding back<br>−Retaliation<br>−Bad attitude<br>−Mind games<br>−Jealousy |
| Expectations | Participants discussing the role of expectations in relationships. | −Participants expectations for their partners<br>−Participants discussing their partners' expectations of them<br>−Collective expectations |
| What's the plan? | Participants discussing their attempts to be planful in the way that they approach their relationships in conjunction with their mate. | −Avoiding pitfalls<br>−Premarital counseling |
| Getting on the same page | Participants discussing their attempts to come to common understanding with partner. | −Love languages<br>−Compatibility<br>−Reaching collective goals |
| Trust | Participants discussing the role of trust in relationships. | −Transparency<br>−No secrets<br>−Infidelity<br>−Being questioned or living under a cloud of suspicion |
| Trauma | Participants discussing the role of trauma or traumatic events in their lives and relationships. | −Physical<br>−Mental/psychological<br>−Relationship |
| Relationship protective factors | Participants discussing attitudes, behaviors, and factors that serve to help relationships. | −Compatibility/ complementary styles<br>−Positive attitude<br>−Respect<br>−Conflict resolution<br>−Working together<br>−Knowing how to be mad or fight fair<br>−Visualizing potential hardship<br>−Being proactive about addressing challenges<br>−Compromise<br>−Intimacy |

(continued)

**Table 2.2.**  *(continued)*

| Code | Description | Branches |
|---|---|---|
| Children | Participants discussing children or the influence of children in/on relationships. | |
| Fatherhood | Participants discussing the role of parenting or fathers and their impact on relationships. | –Participants' own fathers<br>–Participants discussing themselves as fathers<br>–Participants discussing father figures |
| Early relationship experiences | Participants discussing old or previous experiences in relationships. | |
| Peer group/inner circle influences | Participants discussing the role of their peer group in their relationships. | –Peer group marital status<br>–Peer group influences |
| Boundaries | Participants discussing when and how they respected others' intimate relationships. | |
| Self awareness/ reflective | Participants processing life experience in the moment. | |
| Cause for Pause | Participants discussing examples of when they have re-evaluated their intentions. | –Anxiety<br>–Skepticism |
| Growing and evolving in relationships | Participants discussing relationship partners' growth or evolving together as a couple. | –Changing mindset<br>–Solidifying relationship |
| Head vs heart | Participants discussing reconciling or making decisions using either emotion or logic. | –Cost-benefit analysis<br>–Intuition |
| Commitment | Participants discussing the role of commitment or dedication in relationships. | –Investment<br>–Sticking it out<br>–Giving up or quitting too easy<br>–Working at relationships |
| Relationship challenges | Participants discussing environmental relationship stressors. | |
| Make it last forever | Participants romanticizing marriage. | –Long term relationships<br>–Childhood sweethearts |
| Communication | Participants discussing communication patterns in marriage and romantic relationships. | –Honesty<br>–Negative communication<br>–Listening<br>–Compartmentalizing |

| Code | Description | Branches |
|---|---|---|
| Advice | Participants discussing marriage and relationship advice. | –Advice offered by participants<br>–Advice received by participants |
| Gender roles | Participants discussing the role of gender or socially prescribed gender roles in relationships. | –Gender identity<br>–Gender performance<br>–Masculinity/what it means to be a man<br>–Guy code<br>–Egalitarian |
| Preparing for marriage | Participants discussing their individual preparation for marriage. | |
| Life changes | Participants discussing changing circumstances beyond mere relationship transitions. | |
| How couple met/ getting connected | Participants discussing the circumstances surrounding how they entered into relationships. | –Hooking up<br>–One night stand<br>–Sliding vs deciding<br>–Matchmaker intro<br>–Reconnecting<br>–Positioning |
| Health/mental health | Participants discussing the role of health and mental health on their relationships. | |
| Socialization | Participants discussing societal or macro level factors or phenomena impacting their relationships. | –Mainstream<br>–Black culture<br>–Popular culture<br>–Don't go there (topics that are taboo) |
| Perception vs reality | Participants discussing efforts to put up a façade to the outside world to preserve image. | |
| Mentoring/role models | Participants discussing the importance of seeing healthy marriages and romantic relationships. | |
| Me vs we | Participants discussing individual vs collective orientations in relationships. | –Collective unit<br>–Me time<br>–We, not I<br>–Giving space |
| Single life vs on the market | Participants discussing the pros and cons of being single or being willing to engage a romantic relationship. | –Romanticizing being single<br>–Content with being single<br>–Looking for relationship |

(continued)

**Table 2.2.**   *(continued)*

| Code | Description | Branches |
|------|-------------|----------|
| Happiness | Participants discussing how being married or in a romantic relationship impacted happiness. | –Content<br>–Self affirmation |
| Sex | Participants discussing sex or the role of sex in relationships. | |
| Rules of engagement | Participants discussing appropriate behavior when engaging or approaching potential partners. | –How do people date?<br>–Learning to date<br>–Shoot your shot |
| Leadership | Participants discussing the role of leadership and authority in relationships. | –Decision making<br>–Women and independence |
| Finances/ employment | Participants discussing the role of economics in marriage and romantic relationships. | –Work/family balance<br>–Money troubles<br>–Financial provider<br>–Financial stability<br>–White collar vs blue or no collar |
| Religion | Participants discussing the role of religion or spirituality on relationships. | |
| Manhood | Participants discussing the role that marriage and romantic relationships play in shaping masculinity. | |

## STUDY SETTING

Louisville, Kentucky was the setting of *Black Love Matters* and serves as its backdrop. For many reasons, Louisville is an ideal location for an examination of black men's experiences in marriage and romantic relationships. Although Louisville is not as renowned as cities like New York, Chicago, Washington DC, Atlanta, or Los Angeles, the greater Louisville Metro area is home to more than 1 million people and is roughly 25 percent black (U.S. Census Bureau 2017). Moreover, Louisville has a unique history that positioned it as a progressive oasis in a largely conservative region. Put another way, as many locals say, "There's Louisville . . . and then there's Kentucky." Much of this is grounded in Louisville's history as an influential border city in the upper south where slavery existed but the climate did not allow for growing cotton. Therefore, free blacks were reluctantly tolerated. According to Aubespin, Clay, and Hudson's (2011) *Two Centuries of Black Louisville,* the city was an attractive destination for free people of color who had agency and the freedom to migrate, in part because it was one of only a few industrial cities in the south. The result was that throughout its history, blacks in Louisville were able to achieve more than was possible for blacks in communities further south but less than was possible for blacks in cities outside of former slave states.

Post slavery, Louisville played a significant role in the fight for civil rights. A cursory exploration of the city's history reveals several pivotal contributions that had major implications in the fight for equality both locally and beyond. For example, Louisville native, Charles W. Anderson Jr., was the first African American elected to a southern state legislature in the 20th century. Central High School, which had its original curriculum influenced by Booker T. Washington, later became home to other notable educators like Lyman Johnson and still is an exemplar in black public education. The Old Walnut Street Business District was a hub for black economic development that featured restaurants, theaters, insurance companies, and banks. Louisville is also home to historic churches like Quinn Chapel AME and Zion Baptist where Martin Luther King Jr. delivered a notable speech titled, "Upon this Rock" that was instrumental in helping to get an open housing ordinance passed. And perhaps most notably, Louisville's own Muhammad Ali was one of the most outspoken champions for civil rights and equality (Anne Braden Institute n.d). Louisville was also home to protests, riots, and demonstrations in the 1960s and what became known as the "mini Civil war" over the issue of busing in 1975 that tarnished the city's reputation as racially progressive. In the 1980s, a group of black civic and political leaders known as the PAC-10 began organizing in an attempt to pool black political and economic resources. However, the sustained impact of this group was truncated when the city and county governments merged in what many criticized as a plot to dilute black political power (Aubespin and Hudson 2011).

Contemporarily, Louisville has a diverse economy featuring several Fortune 500 corporations in industries including health care, shipping, food services, tobacco, as well as automobile and appliance manufacturing. There are several institutions of higher education in Louisville including the University of Louisville, Bellarmine University, Spalding University, Sullivan University, and the Jefferson County Technical College, as well as numerous cultural, performing arts, and sports attractions. For these reasons, Louisville is known as *Possibility City*. Most importantly, Louisville is a place where many black people are not only surviving but are thriving. Evidence of this is that black men and women are prominent in many public and private sector positions and occupy seats on major decision-making bodies within the city including the chamber of commerce, the University of Louisville Board of Trustees, the Metro Council, the Jefferson County Public Schools Board of

Education, and the Louisville Metro Police Department. Moreover, Louisville is home to several black mega churches, an active chapter of 100 Black Men of America, the National Urban League, Cities United, BMe Community, and hosts the Campaign for Black Male Achievement's annual Rumble Young Man, Rumble event. Each year, many of these high profile blacks are featured in a publication called, "Who's Who in Black Louisville."

Despite the fact that Louisville is a place that boasts a sizeable black middle class and is a place where many black men and women are affluent and influential, it has some challenges that make establishing and maintaining meaningful relationships difficult. These micro and macro factors contribute to disproportionately low socioeconomic, health, and educational outcomes for many blacks. In 2017, the median household income was $61,136 for all Louisvillians and $37,122 for black Louisvillians (U.S. Census Bureau 2017). In 2015, 71 percent of Jefferson County white households were owner occupied compared to only 37.5 percent of black households and in 2016, the median net worth for white college graduates in Louisville was $389,801 and only $65,821 for black college graduates (Jackson 2018). As a result, Louisville is very segregated with blacks making up more than 78 percent of the residents of the west end where 60 percent of them live in poverty, compared to the less than 5 percent of white residents of the east end who live in poverty. These economic and residency differences have significant implications for health disparities between blacks and whites in Louisville. For example, the disproportionately black west end has a gender combined life expectancy of 67 years which is more than a decade shorter than the life expectancy of 82 years in the over 70 percent white east end (Blakely and Little 2018). As it relates to household composition, only 38.5 percent of Louisville's black families are married and 85.3 percent of its single parent households are headed by females (Perry 2018).

Unfortunately, these disparities are not limited to adults. In fact, these gaps are just as pronounced for Louisville's youth. Among small children, 43 percent of black children are kindergarten ready compared to 55 percent of white children. At the elementary school level, 24 percent of black students perform at proficient or above on standardized tests compared to 58 percent of white students. For high schoolers, only 18 percent of all advanced placement exams were taken by black students. Finally, of the 9,000 2- or 4-year degrees conferred in Louisville in 2016, only 12 percent were earned by African Americans (Jackson and Davidson 2018). Black youth make up 29 percent of the youth population but represent 74 percent of the youth detained in Louisville in 2014. Moreover, 50 percent of all black students experience alternative school placement compared to 32 percent of white students (Dawson-Edwards 2018).

In sum, both Louisville's past and present are full of contradictions and juxtapositions. It has been simultaneously a slave state, while also having a reputation for being more benign than other states involved in the peculiar institution. Louisville is often described as progressive, yet it is highly segregated by race. Some of Louisville's most influential residents are black, but the majority of its most marginalized and voiceless citizens are also black. It is in these contradictions and juxtapositions that *Black Love Matters* is situated. It is against the backdrop of widening social, political, educational, and economic outcomes across and within race that the study participants attempt to develop a healthy sense of self in the face of microaggressions and overt discrimination. It is within these divergent environmental contexts that the study participants wrestle with developing and manifesting their own ideas about masculinity while also being influenced by the messages they receive from the world around them about what it means to be a man. It is in this seemingly conflictual space that the study participants work to establish, cultivate, and maintain marriages and romantic relationships.

## THEORETICAL FRAMEWORK

Given the inherent contradictions and juxtapositions that black men have to navigate to establish and maintain romantic relationships and marriages in Louisville, the Theory of Planned Behavior (TPB) provides an appropriate theoretical lens for examining the men's behavior within the contexts of these relationships. TPB was developed by Ajzen (1985) as an extension of the Theory of Reasoned Action (TRA), both of which focus on what motivates an individual to implement a particular behavior (Montano and Kasprzyk 2008). TRA was initially created by Fishbein (1967) to study the connection between an individual's attitudes regarding a behavior, the intention to perform the behavior, and the actual performance of the behavior. In studying the relationships between these three factors, Fishbein found that a person's attitude toward a behavior was predictive of him or her performing that behavior (Fishbein and Ajzen 1975). As with most theories that have been used to explain human behavior, there is an implicit assumption that the behavior is within the person's volitional control or that the individual has control over performing the specific behavior (Montano and Kasprzyk 2008). However, this is not always necessarily the case. Therefore, Ajzen (1991) extended the TRA in order to account for those behaviors that may be outside of a person's volitional control. In doing so, TPB suggests that behavior is not only a function of the intention to perform the behavior, but it is also a function of the individual's ability to perform the behavior (Montano and Kasrzyk 2008).

Although it has been most often applied to quantitative analyses that attempt to explain health behaviors, TPB provides an appropriate lens for examining black men's relationship and marriage behaviors. TPB proposes that human behavior is largely determined by intention and that there are three determinants of intention: attitudes, subjective norms, and perceived behavioral control. Attitudes are a product of the individual's behavioral beliefs about the outcomes of performing a behavior and the evaluation of those behavioral outcomes. Subjective norms are a product of whether an individual believes other meaningful people approve or disapprove of the behavior and their motivation to comply with those people. Lastly, perceived behavioral control is determined by an individual's control beliefs (i.e., whether there are barriers to their control over the behaviors) and the perceived power the individual feels they have over these barriers in order to perform the behavior (Ajzen 1991). Accounting for perceived behavioral control is important because as Ajzen (1988) states,

> The theory assumes that perceived behavioral control has motivational implications for intentions. People who believe that they have neither the resources, nor the opportunities to perform a certain behavior are unlikely to form strong behavioral intentions to engage in it even if they hold favorable attitudes toward the behavior and believe that important others would approve of their performing the behavior. (p. 133)

Thus, TPB allows for a comprehensive analysis of black men's marriage and romantic relationship behavior. This is important because the study participants' narratives not only reveal their attitudes about marriage and romantic relationships, but also shed light on the experiences and circumstances shaping their attitudes and associated behaviors. Therefore, the versatility of TPB in accounting for the intrapersonal (e.g., attitudes and beliefs), interpersonal (e.g., subjective norms or the thoughts of significant others), and the environmental (e.g., community and structural resources or constraints influencing perceptions about volitional control) factors into consideration offer an ideal theoretical framework to guide the data collection and analysis.

## STUDY PARTICIPANTS

Now that the methodological, geographical, and theoretical canvasses have been rolled out, the next section serves to introduce each of the study participants. In an attempt to give voice to black men's lived experiences in marriage and romantic relationships, efforts were made to recruit a diverse sample with regard age, socioeconomic status, educational attainment, family background, and marital status. The following section contains brief demographic profiles for each of the men that includes their pseudonym and demographics (at the time of their initial interview), as well as their responses to questions about their immediate thoughts upon hearing the word *marriage* and a description of their ideal marriage mate. Table 2.3 displays the profiles for each of the study participants at the time of their initial interview.

**Table 2.3.** *Participants' Baseline Profile*

| Name | Age | Relationship Status | Children | Education | Parents' Relationship Status |
|------|-----|---------------------|----------|-----------|------------------------------|
| Alex | 18 | Single | 0 | High School Diploma | Never Married to Each Other |
| Anthony | 19 | Single | 0 | High School Diploma | Never Married to Each Other |
| Rex | 21 | Single (with girlfriend, not serious) | 0 | High School Diploma | Divorced |
| Jeff | 22 | Single (with serious girlfriend) | 0 | College Graduate | Divorced |
| Jake | 22 | Single (with serious girlfriend) | 0 | High School Diploma | Never Married to Each Other |
| Dan | 26 | Single (with girlfriend, not serious) | 0 | College Graduate | Married to Each Other |

| Marriage Word Association | Description of Ideal Marriage Mate |
|---|---|
| Love, two people together. Two people who can't be away from each other, they really like each other and enjoy being in each other's company. . . . Long relationship . . . commitment. Just a long committed relationship. | I don't know. I like all women. I don't really have a type, you know. |
| | Let me start with personality. Personality wise, confidence. I don't want a girl walking around with their head down so I'll always give them compliments so they can feel good. A woman with confidence is very attractive and a woman about her own grind is very attractive. Motivated, intelligent, and willing to learn 'cause there are some smart girls that think they know everything, so being open to learn. . . . Motivated. Either she's taking classes or taking care of her kids, but she's not waiting on a man to come in and help her out. Like if I lose my job, she got one. So, she stays motivated, stays on her feet, and never gets left in the dust and is a little assertive. I don't like little quiet girls, you gotta be able to speak your mind. Far as physical appearance, I like dark skinned girls that are thick. I like natural hair but I'm not too picky about that. |
| Uh . . . lifetime. A lifetime of bonding or a lifetime bond. You know, like you're gonna be with that person your entire life. | I guess I kind of look at that too as far as what kind of mother do I see her being, you know 'cause let's be honest, I'm not getting no younger and it gets harder if you're a successful black male doing your thing. You know how it is. |
| A really long commitment. For the most part, just um. . . . For me, a man and a woman being together for the rest of their lives. | Personality wise . . . I like girls to be humble and meek. Probably . . . I guess self-aware, but not too self-aware. You know, not . . . an unusually bold personality. I just think with me, I think when I can tend to be the bolder of the two, I think that works better. Physically attractive . . . she doesn't have to be you know, gorgeous or anything. I think for the most part like inner beauty is good. |
| To me, to be honest when I hear the word marriage like I think of a wedding. Like the reason why I think of a wedding is because that's . . . I mean because I don't know too many people who last past that. | Well that's simple. I like strong women. Like, I'm not even gonna lie. I like strong women. The type of women where if I was gone tomorrow, she could hold down the household. She could represent me well when I'm not there. . . . Yeah, I mean I have no problem being the man of my house, I have no problem doing that, but I want a woman who being a mother as in . . . if I'm gone for two weeks for my job, I need to know that ain't nothing gonna go out of place and ain't nobody gonna run her ragged. |
| God. Like a church kind of thing. A union, two becoming one, that kind of thing. | Black. Kind of easy going, not real argumentative. Hard working, educated. |

*(continued)*

**Table 2.3.** *(continued)*

| Name | Age | Relationship Status | Children | Education | Parents' Relationship Status |
|------|-----|---------------------|----------|-----------|------------------------------|
| Keith | 27 | Married | 1 | High School Diploma | Never Married to Each Other |
| Ronald | 27 | Single | 0 | High School Diploma | Married |
| Amir | 27 | Married | 1 | GED | Never Married to Each Other |
| Robert | 29 | Married | 3 | High School Diploma | Married (until mother died) |

| Marriage Word Association | Description of Ideal Marriage Mate |
|---|---|
| Marriage. What used to come to mind was aww man [As in you can't be serious], for real. The old me, I guess being younger you know, you want to do what you do, run the streets but as you get older you find that one person that you want to be with. Now what comes to mind is uh . . . it's a experience 'cause I'm married now. It's a experience where you build a foundation, it's what you're going to look forward to, all the things like that. | The kind of women I like man . . . you know what . . . I'm going to start with the physical part I guess. Me, I've always been attracted to shorter women, about 5'5''. My wife is the exception, she's about 5'8'' skinny and petite, but I like the short, thick ones, a little dark skinned for real, you know. Like I say, my wife is the exception. But demeanor, me I try not to be a judgmental person or try not to judge nobody, so I don't really get down with the females that are quote unquote hoes [whores]. I mean, you can . . . I've messed around with a few of them for a jumpoff [casual sex] or whatever, but ultimately relationship wise, you gotta have goals and aspirations 'cause I got goals and aspirations. You gotta want to do something. You gotta be going somewhere 'cause I can do bad by myself. You gotta be willing to work at this thing if we have hard times. You gotta be willing to go hard. |
| Commitment. Being committed to one person. | Mild tempered. I don't like ghetto [laughing]. Everybody is different, but I guess when I think about it, I don't want somebody that I met in a club or anything like that. I don't want a party animal. I want more like a . . . not necessarily a home body, but . . . I don't know the word I'm looking for, just not a party animal. I want someone respectable. |
| Covenant. Well, just that two become one. You know we have some issues about whether certain people get married, but if we called it the covenant of marriage then we wouldn't have any issues with same sex marriage. Because two men can't become one man, so that's why I think about the word covenant. Two becoming one. | Intelligent. Intelligence has always been number 1 on my list. Intelligent and sexy. That's what I always been attracted to. Somebody that can hold a conversation, somebody capable of having a upside. A young lady with some potential. Physically, I think if you look for something sexy, you can find it. It varies 'cause I'm one of those that actually looks for something sexy and then, that's what I hold on to. |
| Uh . . . unity, companionship, love, trust, and wife. | Just like I said the supportiveness and the fact that even though I'm flawed, every man's flawed, every woman's flawed, nobody's perfect but she [participant's wife] looked past all that and saw me for what I was and who I'm capable of being. She's given me her love, I don't have any trust issues with her and at times when I've been down, she's picked me up so for [me] that was major. I've been in quite a few relationships, most of them when I was younger and that's hard to find these days. You know, the fact that she was a young, single black woman, she was about to get her degree, she didn't have any kids and I had two, she was just a diamond in the rough to me. |

*(continued)*

**Table 2.3.** *(continued)*

| Name | Age | Relationship Status | Children | Education | Parents' Relationship Status |
|------|-----|---------------------|----------|-----------|------------------------------|
| Brian | 31 | Married | 1 | High School Diploma | Divorced |
| Wayne | 32 | Single | 0 | College | Never Married to Each Other |
| Sean | 33 | Married | 1 | No High School Diploma, No GED | Never Married to Each Other |

| Marriage Word Association | Description of Ideal Marriage Mate |
|---|---|
| Man and woman, but nowadays with all of the . . . [same sex marriage discourse]. I don't hate on it. It's just that I've always been taught one man and one woman, you know for life, 'til death do us part. | Well man, to be honest I just love women. Race has never been a factor. The mother of my child, she's from Puerto Rico, so race has never been a factor. Personality . . . I love intelligence. Honest to God, there's no bigger turnoff than a woman that's just dingy. She can look great but someone who doesn't know anything or plays the ditzy role, I hate that. What else . . . a person who cares about themselves. You know, cares about how they look. Not saying that they gotta have on the newest clothes all the time but just look like they are put together. I do appreciate that . . . and oh yeah, physical appearance . . . voluptuous women, I ain't gonna lie about that. Skinny, way too skinny is ok but to be honest, I love an ass and some nice breasts. |
| Usually what comes to mind is skepticism a little because like I said before my mother's been married three times. Strike 1, strike 2, strike 3 and it didn't work. My older sister has been married and it didn't work. I've got a brother that's been married, didn't work. I'm looking at all of this and I'm like, why waste the time for real? If it ain't gonna work and you look at all these stats out here saying over 50% or 50% of all marriages end in divorce . . . I'm thinkin' why in the world would I put myself in that position to be married and ultimately end up not being together in the long run? Those are the things that come to my mind. | As far as personality goes, I guess I'd have to have someone who is similar to mine. I guess I'm kind of low key, you know you don't have to be as quiet as I am. I grew up kind of quiet, but I just want somebody who's not so overly aggressive as far as their personality goes. I like somebody who's right in the middle, kind of like me. Somebody who is low key but can have fun but knows you know . . . you know somebody who knows you can't do too much. Personality wise, I like that. Physically, I like . . . I like women who . . . who are . . . [laughing] bigger I guess. I mean full figured. Women . . . it really just depends on the personality. A lot of that has to play into it, but I do like fuller figured women. |
| Commitment. To me when you actually make the step to get married you make a lifetime commitment. And according to Biblical principles, the only thing that can break that commitment is divorce, I mean not divorce, but death or if one of the people has sex with someone else. So, for me, it was something I always wanted but it took me a long time to get. | First of all, she has to have a religious background and believe in the same things I believe in. Outgoing but to herself. By that, I mean that when we're out in public she can have fun with other people but at the same time she don't gossip a lot and is more of a homebody who likes to spend a lot of quality time with the family and with myself and can go to a lot of family events and blend in that environment. Goal oriented and has her own goals that she want to accomplish. Very independent and don't have to depend on anybody but God. Friendly, that's important. In a nutshell, that's it. |

*(continued)*

**Table 2.3.**  *(continued)*

| Name | Age | Relationship Status | Children | Education | Parents' Relationship Status |
|------|-----|---------------------|----------|-----------|------------------------------|
| Terrell | 33 | Married | 0 | High School Dilpoma | Married to Each Other |
| Paul | 34 | Divorced (with a serious girlfriend) | 1 | No High School Diploma | Divorced |

| Marriage Word Association | Description of Ideal Marriage Mate |
|---|---|
| Man and woman being together. You know, we got this pact and we're trying to have this family. First, you gotta have yourself together before they can create a family but if you and your wife ain't together and on the same page, how are you gonna bring your family together . . . first God. Both of them need to be I guess knowing that there is a God, be God fearing and then after that I guess . . . you need to know what y'all are compatible with. What one likes, does the other like? Then after that, I would say financial. I mean can one support the other and does that matter? Then what do y'all want in life? What's the reason for being married? Where are y'all trying to get to, do y'all have a plan? If y'all don't have a plan, how y'all gonna be married? I mean that's what most marriages are supposed to be built on, a plan. If somebody don't have a plan, how y'all gonna succeed? | Uh . . . good humor. I want a woman that works every day, not every day but you know what I mean. A woman that wants good things out of life and is not complacent. Just wants to have motivation to do things and not just wait on me to do everything. I want a woman that has her own little plan that coincides with my plan so we can be on the same path and move straight ahead, you know. A religious person . . . I ain't hard to deal with, you know what I'm saying but one thing I need is a woman that's gonna work 'cause I can't do it all on my own. Plus, if you working then you don't have time for the things that could slide us off the path. If you don't work, there are so many things out here that can captivate you and then you'll lose track of what me and you got going on. I guess that's it though. |
| Forever. . . . When I got married I took it seriously. I did it young, but I took it serious. I feel like if you make that commitment under God, it should be for better or for worse, but the worse didn't get better. There's also a law that states that a man can't divorce a woman unless there's infidelity. Well when you're separated, and you start living like you're in high school, we both started living our own lives, you know. So, when she went out and got another mate, even though we were still legally married, that's when I filed for divorce. | The woman I have now. Now we've had problems, but I like the fire that she has because she's passionate. It's all mixed together, the passion, the love, and she's dependable you know. Sometimes we lose sight of that, but I like a woman with a little powder keg. I don't want a woman that's gonna be all submissive, you know. I want it to be where we walk beside each other and not her walking in front of me or me walking in front of her. So that's the foundation that we've had and so far, so good. I like a strong woman. I love a strong woman because there are a lot of women out here that are not strong because they've been dogged out by so many men. She's experienced that but she's still strong and I've helped to strengthened her to not let me do that to her. |

*(continued)*

**Table 2.3.** *(continued)*

| Name | Age | Relationship Status | Children | Education | Parents' Relationship Status |
|------|-----|---------------------|----------|-----------|------------------------------|
| Peter | 35 | Married | 1 | College | Married to Each Other |
| Quincy | 37 | Divorced | 3 | College | Never Married to Each Other |
| Reggie | 37 | Divorced (with girlfriend, not serious) | 2 | High School Diploma | Never Married to Each Other |

| Marriage Word Association | Description of Ideal Marriage Mate |
|---|---|
| I'd say love. You've got to have love for a marriage to work. The second thing is partnership. You know when you get married you take on . . . you're taking on someone else's beliefs, you're taking on their family, you're taking on their habits whether they're good or bad and you have to mingle that with your situation because you become one. The old me died when I got married and that doesn't mean that the old me was a bad person, but I couldn't continue with the same lifestyle, mentality, everything when I got married. The same thing for my wife. You know we entered into a new partnership, a new thing, it's a whole new ball game. | Well, I think we had a lot alike. A lot of things we liked to do together. We both were from the country, it's amazing that we'd never met, but a lot of the interests we had were in common. Well like the tv shows we like. Um . . . musical interests even though she's a little bit more diverse than me. We made each other laugh and enjoyed each other's company. We just really liked to be around one another. |
| Um . . . not a destination. That is normally the first thing that comes to mind. Especially young people, when they talk about getting married, they talk about it like it's the end. Like it's the end of the process when it's really the middle or the beginning of a brand new process. I think that line of thinking is. Thinking that once you get married, everything will get better, everything will change. Now everything does change but it doesn't mean it gets better. It may be a different set of problems . . . and to make it last, you've got to be willing to put in the work to make it last. | I don't have a preference on physical appearance, but I guess somebody that's laid back, easy to talk to and can hold their own in a debate. And somewhat opinionated. I don't like meek, hold their own opinion type women. If you think I'm wrong, please tell me I'm wrong and have reasons why, not just because you said so [laughing]. Now I may eventually admit that I was wrong, but first I want to see how strong your argument is. |
| Uh . . . two people I guess . . . making a life commitment. Two people who are in love with each other. I don't know . . . | Uh . . . I feel like I got somebody who genuinely care about me and will go to bat for me and my kids. You know, I mean if I call her right now and need her, as soon as she gets out of surgery, she'll be on the way. She's what I like to call a ride or die chick regardless of whatever and they're hard to find. Some of 'em out here, they'll start out doing stuff, but their motive is to reel you in and then the tables turn. I need this, I need that bill paid and I ain't trying to be no sugar daddy. I took care of one for 13 years and after our divorce, she still wasn't pleased. |

*(continued)*

**Table 2.3.** *(continued)*

| Name | Age | Relationship Status | Children | Education | Parents' Relationship Status |
|------|-----|---------------------|----------|-----------|------------------------------|
| Nick | 43 | Single (engaged to be married) | 2 | College | Married to Each Other (until father died) |
| Adam | 45 | Divorced (with girlfriend, not serious) | 4 | High School Diploma | Married to Each Other |
| Josh | 46 | Married | 10 | High School Diploma | Never Married to Each Other |

| Marriage Word Association | Description of Ideal Marriage Mate |
|---|---|
| Um . . . you know, support . . . support for one another. I'll say in all ways whether its mentally, spiritually, physically, emotionally. Those are probably the first things that come to mind when I think about marriage based on what I saw with my mother and father. | Uh . . . [laughing] you know, that's a damn good question. Temperament, I like intelligent women from a standpoint that they are well rounded and not just book smart, who are just not street smart, who are just not world news smart, but have everything. They gotta have a little edge. For lack of a better term, I don't want them to be no punk. I don't like women who are yes dear, yes dear 'cause I ain't like that. I keep hearing some brothers say that you gotta be like that, but I can't be like that. I don't want a woman who says yes just because I said it. If you have an opinion, then let's talk about it. We may not even agree on it. I like women like that, a woman who knows who she is. Most of the women I've dated have been above average height, between 5'6"–5'7". My youngest daughter's mom is not tall so she's the exception. Uh . . . I like women who have a natural beauty, not a lot of makeup and hair extensions and all that stuff. I just like them to be . . . attractive from a purely natural standpoint. And none of the women that I've dated look anything alike. |
| Unity and togetherness. I say togetherness because when I think about marriage, I think about family. I think about living together, eating together, praying together, laughing together, crying together. Unity and togetherness is also about just being together, you know. It's about supporting each other. | Me, I like patient women, I like spiritual women, but I don't really have a type of women as far as what she looks like though. I've dated a lot of different types of women and I'm to a point where I realize that that [physical appearance] is a shell and I'm more concerned with people's spirit and the way they treat me. |
| Before I got married, every person that I knew who was married, everything was negative. I never had one person to say something positive about marriage. Maybe I wasn't around it enough. Now I wasn't questioning it like you [conducting a study with marriage as the topic], I was just listening on the side 'cause I was about to get married. | [Laughing] As a animal, it is bad knowing and having the knowledge that I have now knowing that it was animal instincts. All my women were chosen off purely physical 'cause I like short women, real petite women. My wife was real young and people will be like, man you're like R. Kelly but I just liked petite, small women when I went back and looked but through the teaching and me learning, I remembered that a lady who kept me while my mother was working, Jannie, she was real short and real petite. She was real mean to me, she would beat on me and stuff and I would recall it in my mind so maybe I would acquire short women and mistreat them over my span without even thinking about it. I heard a brother once say that men get women like their mother and this lady was a prominent person in my life and . . . just a little self analyzation that I've done. |

*(continued)*

**Table 2.3.** *(continued)*

| Name | Age | Relationship Status | Children | Education | Parents' Relationship Status |
|---|---|---|---|---|---|
| Thomas | 47 | Divorced | 4 | College | Never Married to Each Other |
| Chad | 50 | Divorced and Remarried | 3 | High School Diploma | Never Married to Each Other |
| Brandon | 53 | Married | 2 | High School Diploma | Married |
| Vince | 58 | Married | 5 | College | Married (until both died) |

| Marriage Word Association | Description of Ideal Marriage Mate |
|---|---|
| Covenant, two people working together to have a wholesome relationship and to raise children that are healthy, functional, productive members of society. Covenant, two people working together to have a wholesome relationship and to raise children that are healthy, functional, productive members of society. | Um . . . a woman who can trust. 'Cause ultimately if a person can't trust you, then they can't respect you. So, first trust, respect, and uh . . . a woman that's honest about if she has trust issues to put that on the table. Again, it would probably not be a relationship I would get into if a woman has challenges trusting but then if that did come up after the marriage commitment, her being willing to get the necessary counseling to work through those issues and ultimately develop trust. That would be important. |
| I guess having a partner. Fulfilling what God has instructed us to do for the betterment of man and society. That's what I think about. More so from a personal perspective, it's about having a partner, someone that I can depend on and help me make it through life and other social things. | I like intelligent women. I like women that can articulate where they are and who they are. I like women that I can talk to, that can give me feedback, that can help me be a better me. Uh . . . then from a standpoint of the mind first, but then from a physical standpoint, if I see their hair then I'm open. The second thing is how they relate from a brain standpoint is where I go. |
| Well uh . . . it was designed to be about love so that is the first thing that comes to mind and that's what I'm looking for in it. | It's about the personality for me. It's about having a good personality and being wise by using it and being loving. I like intelligent and loving women. Anything else misses the mark. |
| When I hear the word marriage, what comes to mind for me is a man and woman that have made a union and a promise to take on life together. | Oh, I've always felt I needed to base myself in marriage 'cause I married one woman twice. I always wanted to be . . . if I had a child, I wanted to be in that child's life. I thought that would make things better for them than I had it, see my daddy kind of walked when I was younger, so I told myself it's easier to tackle things with two [parents]. See when I grew up in the 60s, men went out and worked and the women stayed home and raised the children. It was tough for them to find a job anyway unless they were working in somebody's house for white people. So, at 18 when you got out of high school, the girls was looking for a husband and the guys was looking to dodge the draft, you know. But my girl was pregnant and I didn't have any insurance and I didn't want my child brought into this world by a midwife. So, one day I was walking down the street and I saw this poster of Uncle Sam and it said, I want you. And so, I felt like he was talking to me, that was a way I could take care of my obligations as a man so that's what I decided to do. |

*(continued)*

**Table 2.3.** *(continued)*

| Name | Age | Relationship Status | Children | Education | Parents' Relationship Status |
|------|-----|---------------------|----------|-----------|------------------------------|
| John | 59 | Divorced | 2 | High School Diploma | Married to Each Other |
| Chris | 60 | Married | 3 | Graduate School | Divorced |
| William | 60 | Divorced and Remarried | 3 | College | Married |

| Marriage Word Association | Description of Ideal Marriage Mate |
|---|---|
| Uh . . . comfort. I think having grown up in a two parent household and having seen a marriage work through its ups and downs over the years and the fact that my upbringing was fairly comfortable, that's the reason why I bring up the word comfort. | I tend to like women who are strong . . . well self-confident, they know where they want to go and have the skill set to do it. And uh, I don't like clingy women and they fit the mold. And even on the look thing, they were different looks. One was short and the other was taller. They're both black but the second one was more built like a model. You know, beyond that I don't know that there was anything in common. I just liked the fact that they were both women I could deal with on the same level. The first one, she is a little spicy so that was interesting and intriguing so that fit in with my earlier years. The second one was, I was just taken by the way she carried herself and where her head was on some issues, that kind of thing. Of course, in both cases I needed to look deeper because the devil is under the covers and it's a matter of what devil you can tolerate. |
| Biblically, two become one. And meaning one physically and in the sense of two people in the arena of their emotions and obviously spiritually. | I think faithfulness is very important to me. I definitely have to have a woman that I feel like I can trust. Of course, by faithful to me I mean that I'm her only man. Financially, I expect that she have some self-discipline about herself and it is important that she want a family. It became increasingly important as we grew in our faith that she valued the same things in faith that I valued in our walk with the Lord. That has really been the glue that has held us together for 36 years. |
| Family. Community. To me, marriage is about family and how to build families, strong families. And of course, strong families at least in my opinion, strong families are the foundation of strong communities. Marriage or being married is what legitimizes family and solidifies marriage. Now I'm a little older but where I'm from, a family isn't really a family unless it is headed by a married couple, that's the stabilizing factor. It's the thing that stabilizes the family, you know. That's when the community can recognize the family. | I wanted a college educated woman, a woman with similar interests and values. Somebody who I could take to different events in the community and talk to about world views and stuff, you know. My expectations have changed over time. I have changed and so what I'm looking for changed so like I said as I got older, I wanted to find somebody who matched where I was at the time. When I was younger, I didn't really have no expectations, I didn't even think about expectations. My first wife was only my second relationship if you can even call it a relationship, so I didn't have a lot of experience with women before, you know. Oh yeah, another thing about it is that I tend to have a overshadowing kind of personality, so it's important to me have someone who will let me be me, you know. Like, I can't be with someone trying to change who I am. |

*(continued)*

**Table 2.3.** *(continued)*

| Name | Age | Relationship Status | Children | Education | Parents' Relationship Status |
|------|-----|---------------------|----------|-----------|------------------------------|
| Michael | 61 | Divorced | 3 | College | Married to Each Other |
| Andrew | 62 | Married | 2 | Graduate School | Married to Each Other |
| Tim | 63 | Married | 4 | College | Never Married to Each Other |

| Marriage Word Association | Description of Ideal Marriage Mate |
|---|---|
| I think its uh, I know it has to be someone who cares. It has to be two people coming together and like you say, I don't believe in how you say . . . I made the mistake, I had a child out of wedlock, but you try to not keep making the same mistake. I uh, tell young men and women too 'cause I have daughters. Try to be married and try to give yourself when you get married, but don't go out and uh . . . you know have five and six children or have sex anytime you can without being married. | Well uh, I think more so, the only way I know how to explain it is, I know I like, it's not about being the perfect cook or anything like that. I like people that treat me the same at home as they do in public. If they see me doing something wrong, don't front me out please. Just pull me over to the side and say hey, don't do that or just tap me on the shoulder. Don't be like, NIGGA! You know how some people, men and women are . . . loud like that. |
| Uh . . . commitment, team, partnership you know. Mutuality, common interests, shared goals and aspirations. | Well I've been married for over 30 years, so I better say I like those characteristics to fit her [participant's wife] in case it gets back to her [laughing]. What would attract me if I could do it all over again in retrospect . . . um . . . I guess a measure of physical attractiveness but that isn't the main thing. A temperament, a measure of what I would perceive as similar life goals and expectations. Similar dreams and a sense that we want to go to the same place, we want to travel the same road or at least that perception. That's probably one reason why people end up divorced is because they find out they're on separate roads and going in different directions so I'm sure that contributes to it. |
| A legal system of bonding. | Intelligent, good communication skills . . . uh not too fat, not too skinny. . . . As far as behavior, adventurous. Willing to travel. Able to exist in various and different cultures. Like, you know, my wife is from DC for example. And so . . . you know she is like able to you know, I can take her different places, wherever I want to. And she can pretty much fit in. She's not intimidated. She doesn't . . . she knows how to culturally deal with different things. |

*(continued)*

**Table 2.3.** *(continued)*

| Name | Age | Relationship Status | Children | Education | Parents' Relationship Status |
|------|-----|---------------------|----------|-----------|------------------------------|
| Joe | 64 | Married | 2 | High School Diploma | Married to Each Other (until they died) |
| Tyrone | 72 | Divorced and Remarried | 2 | Graduate School | Divorced |

| Marriage Word Association | Description of Ideal Marriage Mate |
|---|---|
| Commitment . . . commitment to each other. Just doing the right thing 'cause uh . . . I was 17 when we got married, but the reason we got married was because my wife became pregnant so getting married was the right thing to do. You know, I was brought up in the church all my life, so we got married. | She was just my girlfriend at that time, so I don't know if anything set her apart. We hung out together, you say love, but I don't know if that's what it was at that age, so we had to grow up together. Now, you couldn't separate us. We do everything together. The older we get, the stronger the bond is. We think the same. You can ask her the same questions as me and she would answer it the same way as I would. It's just our character or personalities are mended because marriage or any type of relationship, it's give and take. We give a lot, we take a lot, but we don't let anything come between us. |
| Family, interdependency, and love | I don't really have a list. It's kind of just something where you kind of go with the flow. Obviously, I'd like for them to be intelligent, to dress well. Not, not . . . just know how to wear clothes. You know, some women don't know how to wear clothes in my opinion. Able to carry on a conversation with them and have fun with them. It could be going to a basketball game, walking on the beach, going to a play or just sitting around the house laughing, joking or having friends over. |

## CONCLUSION

The purpose of this chapter was to set the stage for the remainder of *Black Love Matters*. To do so, details regarding the study methods, geographical setting, and guiding theoretical framework, as well as the men themselves have been provided. This behind the scenes look into the study's conceptualization, its participants, and the city in which it took place contextualizes and frames the subsequent chapters. In these chapters, the men's narratives are featured, and their lived experiences are highlighted through the use of direct quotes and firsthand accounts. Although the men's discussions cover myriad topics, specific emphasis is placed on the role of sex in marriage and romantic relationships, the impact of previous traumas in shaping the men's relationship experiences, the men's relationship transitions and trajectories over time, and the extent to which the men's identities are shaped by their romantic relationships. *Black Love Matters* concludes with a final chapter dedicated to a discussion of the lessons learned and relationship and marriage advice that the men offer to those concerned with black male-female romantic relationships.

## Chapter Three

# Let's Talk about Sex

## with Dr. Cheri Langley

Much like broader discussions of black marriage and male-female relationships, public discourse and academic research on black men's sexual attitudes and behavior tend to be deficit framed. Historical stereotypes and controlling images that have negative implications in contemporary contexts persist. Throughout their residence in the United States, black men's sexuality has been framed as violent, dangerous, and predatory (Anderson 1990; Collins 2002; Kniffley, Brown, and Davis 2018). During slavery, fears of insurrection which were assumed would include large numbers of rapes were used to justify formal and informal laws, policies, and customs to restrict black men's activity and mobility. Post slavery, newspapers, books, and racialized "science" all became venues for pathologizing black men's sexuality, paving the way for racial violence, usually in the form of lynching (McGruder 2010). In many ways, these stereotypes and controlling images were crystalized in D. W. Griffith's *Birth of a Nation*, a film that the Ku Klux Klan used as recruitment propaganda as it featured scenes in which white men in blackface lustily hunted down white women in an attempt to sexually assault them (Jones 2005). The result was the stereotype of the black man as virile, hypersexual, and uncontrollable that continues to persist in contemporary society (Childs, Laudone, and Tavernier 2010).

Hooks (2004) and others (Neal 2005) assert that black males learn from an early age that they live in a society that has no room for men seen as sensitive and instead forces them to be cool and dangerous, bad boys. Most often, this is explained as the result of negative economic shifts and disproportionately high incarceration rates that have rocked the financial fortunes of many black men, heightening the need for these alternative masculinities (e.g. hypersexual, predatory) for some men. So pervasive are these notions of black men as hypersexual and predatory that they have been cast as dogs in public discourse. As explained by Benjamin (2014), the negative epithet of the dog is applied by women to explain the behavior of men who fail to fulfill their prescribed ideal role of breadwinner, companion, husband, and father. Typically, women do not perceive men's inability to fulfill traditional roles as a function of external forces (i.e. racism and restricted opportunities); hence they use the dog stereotype to rationalize any conflicts and shortcomings that occur between them. Moreover, the literature indicates that some black women may also perceive black men as passive, unreliable, irresponsible, unfaithful, less likely to contribute, and less committed to long-term romantic relationships (Bell, Bouie, and Baldwin 1990; Bell 1999; Cazenave and Smith 1990; Lawrence-Webb, Littlefield, and Okundaye 2014). Further exacerbating these issues is that since black women's sexuality has also been stereotyped and deficit framed, some black men may see women who are sexually assertive as promiscuous, assuming that her freedom with him means that she is sexually free with other men as well (Crook, Thomas, and Cobia 2009).

Indeed, insidious sexual stereotypes shape the way that many black men and women see themselves and each other. The impact of these stereotypes contributes to relationship and communication problems and also impair couples' ability to develop honesty and trust (Cazenave and Smith 1990). Given the centrality of sex in shaping relationship trajectories and outcomes, exploring the men's sexual attitudes and behaviors is integral to better understanding their perspectives and experiences. In discussing their perceptions and experiences, 31 of the 33 (93.9%) interview participants discussed the ways in which sex shapes marriage and romantic relationships. In sharing their narratives, there were several emergent themes. These themes included some cursory discussions related to the role of religion in the men's sexual attitudes and behaviors, as well as the broader socialization around sex that the men experienced. In addition to religion and cultural socialization, the most prominent themes were related to casual sex versus sex in committed relationships, the influence of media, sex and faithfulness, and the role that sex does or does not play in achieving intimacy.

## RELIGION AND SEXUAL SOCIALIZATION

With regard to the role of religion, it was invoked in a number of different contexts including the imperatives on both responsibility and morality. In recalling a phrase coined by his mother to describe men who fathered children and did not provide for them, Joe, a retired 64-year-old married father of two adult children, also talked about how the Bible provides instructions for how one should comport themselves:

> We got a lot of breath in britches. They just don't understand what a man's re-
> sponsibility is. A lot of the guys just don't understand what their responsibility is
> to family, to kids. They just walk around and say, hey man I got five babies. That's
> not a man. Who takes care of them? Do you work? Things like that, they have
> no idea what their responsibilities are. If they go to the Bible they can find out.

Here, "breath in britches" is used as a pejorative to describe men who engage
in sexual activity but do not take responsibility for the children born out of
their sexual activity. In other instances, the men talked about religion from
a moral standpoint. This perspective is highlighted by Sean, an unemployed
33-year-old married father, who offered the following:

> And how God said it's more important than anything because having sex outside
> of marriage is immoral and can actually lead you down the road of destruction
> which I was a part of at one point in time myself . . . I used to think that if I had
> a boy, I would raise him up like I came up. I would tell him to have sex if he
> wanted and mess with whoever you want to just make sure you protect yourself,
> but now I'm not even on that no more. The Bible says raise up a child in the way
> that he should go and even when he gets older and begins to think for himself,
> he won't fall too far away from that. So now I have to teach my sons that it's ok
> to not have sex until you're married because that's a principle that God honors
> and stand by that, then they will be better off than I was because they will have
> had someone to teach them better, you know.

Sharing this perspective, Sean discusses the role of religion in shaping his
sexual attitudes. In doing so, he reflects on his younger days when he was
more accepting of premarital sex, but in his current state of mind, he has
become more religious and is interested in instilling these values in his son.

In addition to the discussion related to the role of religion, the men also
talked frequently about their broader socialization around sex. When this
came up, it was usually within the context of cultural socialization. Specifically, there were several men who talked about the pressure they felt from
family and friends to formalize their relationships. In other words, there was a
presumption that they were having sex with everyone that they dated. Therefore, many black men and women feel compelled to rush into a "relationship"
to avoid the stigma of having casual sex outside of an established romantic
relationship, particularly if such behavior is frowned upon or stigmatized in
their circles of influence. As such, this pressure created a tension that is sometimes difficult to negotiate or navigate. For example, Dan, a single 26-year-
old pastor, talked about the teaching he received from his father:

> Sometimes with black people, we think every person that we bring around—you
> don't want them to think that you're having sex with all of them. You want to

be real considerate of their feelings, and that's why you only bring certain ones. I remember my father telling me as a child, there are certain girls that you date out there in the street, and there are the ones you bring home to your mother.

This perceived pressure to formalize their relationships came up in other interviews and was corroborated by several participants including Paul, a divorced 34-year-old poet and actor who stated, "Right. Because there's this sort of internal pressure within the culture to put people together before they're really ready." Beyond the discussions related to religion and broader socialization around sex within black culture, sex and its impact on marriage and romantic relationships also emerged in several other contexts. These themes were labeled casual sex vs sex in committed relationships, sex and influence of media, as well as sex, fidelity, and intimacy—that may or may not include sex.

## Casual Sex vs Sex in Committed Relationships

Some of the liveliest conversations that we had with the men were those surrounding the topic of casual sex versus sex within a committed romantic relationship or marriage. In sharing their perspectives, there were strong feelings on all sides of the issue. In sharing his favorable attitudes on casual sex Amir, a 27-year-old married father stated, "Cause like when you're not married, you're not fully committed so why act like it." This sentiment was shared by several other men. Among those considered to be squarely in the pro casual sex camp was Josh, a 46-year-old small business owner and former pimp with 10 children, who recalls meeting the woman he later married cruising around town looking to *hook up*.

I had intentions, when I met her, I tease her all the time, I was riding up Broadway, [she] was on the bus stop, I asked [her] if you need a ride. I told her when I picked her up, I'm just trying to fuck. It was just like that and I was damn near like stalking 'cause she's 10 years younger than me. She was 17 and I was 27 so I'm stalking, trying to get some pussy. [She] gonna get in the car, [she] don't even know me. [She] in the car with a stranger. . . . What's [her] part? When I met her she was on the bus stop. I wanted some ass. You know, you look up at your life, how did I get here? But didn't nobody put me here, it was all choices that I made.

Here, Josh openly discusses how when he met his now wife, he had no intentions to establish a long-term relationship. Instead, as he states quite plainly, he simply wanted to engage in casual sex. This comment is representative of about one-third of the men we interviewed as they recounted times in their lives where they readily and willingly engaged in casual sex. Interestingly, also much like Josh who mentions looking up at his life and pondering how he got there, for many of the men, these causal sexual encounters somehow morphed into relationships. Most often when this happened, the men implicated their female partners as the party initiating or pursing the formal relationship. For example, in our original interview with Jake, a 22-year-old college student, he shared some of his experiences, offering the following:

> But to be honest a lot of them were lying the entire time because a lot of women come in your life and they say they just want to be friends then they sleep with you before the end of the week. Then all of a sudden, it's like, you said you just wanted to be friends and now you want to be committed and I'm like, naw that's not what we discussed. A girl can have platonic friends until y'all have sex and then that's when the line is crossed. Once you sleep with the guy, he may be perfectly ok with just being friends, but she starts to develop feelings. I just realized this about a month ago, because before I didn't understand why all these women were telling me that they just wanted to be friends when really, without being vulgar, they just wanted to mess around. And ultimately, they wanted a commitment, but it's a problem when you're like that's what you told me you don't want because if I had known, I wouldn't have messed with you in the first place. So, it's like with women that have been in my life, I would be like, you have ulterior motives. You knew that once we messed around, you would catch feelings.

Similar to Jake, Tim, a 63-year-old married father and computer analyst, discussed how in his experience, some of the women that he had casual sex with developed feelings for him, seemingly overnight.

> I mean, it's like you go and deal with a girl and wake up in the morning after sex and it's like she's a different person . . . [laughing] come on now, you know what I'm talkin' about! I'm just sayin' that's the way it goes down most of the time, because they think that sex, when you start having sex with them, everything is supposed to be different. Why? It's just sex. You see, they want to confuse sex with love. Man, those are two different animals. . . . But it's like I said, a lot of women get confused. Don't get me wrong, men get confused too, but women get confused more than men.

Although women were implicated more often than men as being susceptible to *catching feelings*, as Tim mentions, it happens to men as well. In fact, Paul talked in great detail about how falling into a "relationship" can be one of the pitfalls of casual sex as he opened up about a romantic relationship that he developed with a woman who he originally considered to be a friend after having a sexual encounter with her. On a related note, Paul also shared with us the ways that engaging in casual sex contributed to a great deal of consternation with regard to his perception of his partners.

If I meet a female and we happen to hook up I'll probably [have sex with her], it wouldn't bother me . . . I don't like that about myself. I really would like to meet a female who would actually interest me in courting her. Not giving it to me so fast. I wished that she would make me wait. I always told myself if it got to be before two weeks this is not the one. I always knew that. Now as I get older, I look at it and I'm like, you know what, if a woman made me wait and actually made me pursue her, I would probably respect that more. A month or whatever, 90 days. That would signal to me that she has a little bit more pride about herself. She respects herself a whole lot more. . . . [However,] I really can't judge them because some of them have very good jobs. Some of them are nurses. I dated a lawyer and a doctor, but it was physical from jump. For one, I convinced her to let me have it quick. The way I feel about it sometimes is like they have this attraction to me, and I have it to them and we did what we did. Me going by my past, it's a double-edged sword. I want to sleep with her so it shouldn't matter or whatever. It's kind of a double-edged sword because I can't be judgmental when we both wanted the same thing.

Here Paul is conflicted as he attempts to make sense of the complicated nature of his relationships. Specifically, he is trying to balance respecting his female partners' sexual agency with the seemingly natural inclination to default to misogynist and sexist double standards grounded in judgement. It is reminiscent to a cat and mouse game where simultaneously, Paul wants to have sex with his female partners and works to convince her to have sex with him only to admit that the very act made him lose respect for her and decreased the probability that he would enter into a relationship with her. In the process, he even suggests that the he would respect the women more if they invoked an artificial probationary period before having sex with him. In doing so, he specifically suggests a month or 90 days, perhaps a reference to Harvey's guidelines from *Act Like a Lady*. Either way, the quote serves to support Tim's theory that both men and women are susceptible to catching feelings, intentionally or unintentionally, when they engage in casual sex. As we learn in chapter 5, this becomes a pattern for Paul who enters and exits multiple relationships across the study period, many of them starting with a casual sexual encounter.

Another finding related to casual sex was its relationship with the concepts of truth and honesty. For these men, causal sex was fine as long as they were open and honest about it. To be specific, some of the men posited honesty and transparency as a rationale to justify engaging in casual sex and in some extreme cases, even infidelity. Here, in his initial interview, Josh describes how the emphasis that he placed on transparency and honesty almost compelled him to confess his infidelity to his son.

I'm such a truthful person. I tell it like it is. I don't put no cut on nothing, so . . . I'm just straight up. I remember with my young son, he's nine now but before I got married, I would be about to go out so he was probably like a newborn and he would say, "Daddy what you getting ready to do" and I was getting ready to go get my dick sucked and I was damn near ready to say it to the baby because this is just how truthful I was, but that was one of the things that was leaning me towards . . . man you gotta stop doing this, you know. Just going out and doing whatever men do in the street 'cause even then she was just a girlfriend or fiancée or whatever, I hadn't married her yet, but I knew what I was doing was wrong.

Much like Josh, in one of Sean's early interviews, he discussed how before settling down, he juggled several different relationships simultaneously. However, unlike Josh who concedes that despite his transparency, acknowledged what he was doing was wrong, Sean makes no such concession, but does make a point to mention that he was always truthful about his relationships.

Even then it seems like I was still trying to find which one can be that one for me. At the same time with my daughter's mom. I want to go out. I want different women. Even though my [daughter's] mom might want to go out with me. It's like I always wanted to have that one but at the same time just the situation dictated there was always something else. Even though when I do, they knew I had my daughter's mom. I never lied. If one were to ask I'd be like, "Yup, I'm with my daughter's mom. We're blah, blah, blah. We live together. I take care of the household. She take care of the household." Am I going to marry her? No, I'm not. Women, they accepted that. They be like trying to find out which one was the one I was going to be with at that time.

However, in other cases, the truth and honesty were presented not as a rationale to justify bad behavior but as a way of recognizing and acknowledging what many of the men claimed to already know or at least believe—that for many women, their participation in casual sex oftentimes leads to feelings of emotional attachment. Consider Jeff's statement below.

Recognizing that even the toughest of women are sensitive. No matter [what] . . . your promiscuity of being with other women, all that affects how they view the next relationship. I think, in a line of cases, just say that you will date her. If you decide that you don't want to be in a relationship, just tell her you don't want to be in a relationship. Rather than this whole sort of having your cake and eating it too. If you say, Hey, I like you but . . . I think that's more genuine and more honest. Be honest. Don't be a dick. Don't lie. Be honest with where you are in the relationship. How you are feeling about how it's going. I found, for the most part, when I told women something, they believed me. They genuinely took you at your word and that's a dangerous thing.

Here Jeff, who was a 22-year-old recent college graduate who was engaged to his long term girlfriend at the time of his initial interview, encourages other men to be honest with themselves and their partners about where they stand in their relationships. In sharing this, he mentions the potential damage and lasting effects that can be done when women are mistreated in their relationships, a story that many of our men know all too well as we find out in chapter 4.

Consistent with Jeff, nearly two-thirds of the men steadfastly rejected the notion of casual sex. The following excerpt is from Terrell, a 33-year-old married man. In his initial interview, he discussed how even before got married, he was more selective than others around him.

> Like most women, they think on the first date you're supposed to take 'em to the mall, take 'em out to eat, take 'em to the club and then after that, it's on. But me, I'd rather take you out to eat, go to a club and then we might split for the rest of the night, know what I'm saying? We ain't gotta be all up under each other 'cause it will probably come to a point where somebody will want some sex and I don't get down on the first date 'cause I'm a picky person.

For some men, their rejection of casual sex was about the emphasis they placed on reserving sex for marriage. Most often, these sentiments were expressed by older men. William, a 60-year-old remarried non-profit administrator and father of three, discussed reserving sex for marriage from the standpoint that it linked to several positive familial and relationship outcomes.

> Marriage is important if you're going to have children. I wanted children and to raise them the proper way and be successful in life. I wanted some stability. There's sexual stability, also. You've committed to somebody, and you don't have to go out looking for sex every time you want to have sex, and all the drama resulting from that. Overall, it's a wonderful institution. It's a healthy institution. Married men tend to live longer.

Similar to William, Michael, a 61-year-old remarried father, also invoked his children as his rationale for rejecting premarital sex.

> I uh, tell young men and women too 'cause I have daughters, try to be married and try to give yourself when you get married, but don't go out and uh . . . you know have five and six children or have sex anytime you can without being married, you know? Respect it because it's a part of life, but it [sex] should be in a marriage.

In addition to citing favorable familial outcomes or personal reasons like being picky as reasons for refraining from casual sex, some of the other men evolved to a point where casual sex no longer had the appeal that it once had.

This was a popular perspective and was best expressed by John, a 59-year-old divorced radio account executive who stated:

> Yeah, so when I got to college, I was like wow this is a playground. I'm going to have a good time. So, I think I went from player to dog for a while there. Then post college that continued for a period of about 10 years until I reached a level a maturity where I was like, come on now, this is getting old. You know the clubbin', the women, you know it just got old.

Clearly, whether or not to engage in casual sex represented a major decision for the men in our study. In many ways, the decision to either endorse and engage or reject and refrain was a distinguishing factor separating the men into two very different factions. Closely related to whether or not the men subscribed to the idea that sex should occur exclusively within the context of a committed relationship, namely marriage, was that the relationship between sex and faithfulness took center stage. Therefore, next we provide a more detailed discussion of the men's experiences and perspectives on sex and faithfulness.

## Sex and Fidelity

Closely related to the men's discussions on the merits of casual sex versus sex in committed relationships or marriage were the men's discussions focused on sex and fidelity. In offering these perspectives, the men discussed infidelity as a function of being cheated on and being unfaithful themselves, infidelity as an ever-present threat to relationships, and the ways in which the threat of retaliatory infidelity served to foster faithfulness.

Perhaps the most damaging of all the experiences that the men discussed was having to deal with the being cheated on. Several of the men we interviewed dealt with this and for many, it changed the trajectory of the relationship they were in at the time. For others, the deleterious effects of infidelity not only impacted the relationships that they were in at the time, but it also negatively impacted their willingness to pursue them into the future, a topic that is highlighted in chapter 4 as it focuses on the impact of trauma (including trauma borne out of previous negative relationship experiences). Here, we amplify how the men spoke specifically about the impact of infidelity on their relationships. First, we have Wayne, who was 32 years old and single at the time of his initial interview, as he shares how his relationship with his ex-girlfriend deteriorated and eventually ended with her being unfaithful.

> Ok um . . . for me, I guess this is my big thing. One of the biggest things for me is about respect. That plays a big part in what I look for in relationships you

know because it usually starts out all good, but it usually ends up you know for some odd reason it gets a little disrespectful you know. I'm really not sure why because I haven't sat down and really analyzed it and think about what went on. But one of the things I've come to expect is mutual respect and I don't want that to ever ever end no matter if we're arguing or not. 'Cause usually when they start being disrespectful, I see that as the beginning of the end to me because that leads to other things. Disrespect leads to more disrespect leads to somebody cheating and stepping out because . . . you know, she doesn't see you in the same light as she does before and you know, you think the grass is greener.

Here, Wayne reflects on what he calls the beginning of the end of his relationship with the girlfriend he had before our first interview with him. The experience of being cheated on, combined with the fact that several members of his family had gone through divorce made him reluctant to enter into another serious relationship. For years, Wayne refused to commit to an exclusive relationship. As we learn in chapter 5, it was only when an old friend resurfaced did he even consider having a serious girlfriend who he subsequently married. Like Wayne, Rex, a single 21-year-old college student, also bore the unfortunate burden of having to bounce back after being cheated on. However, unlike Wayne, over the years, Rex moved in and out of several relationships but none of them were sustainable, in part, due to the trust issues that he developed as a result of being cheated on. Rex explains below:

Things went really well, and we were really clicking, but I guess I'll say you let me know if you need me to expound upon anywhere there, but kind of long story short about it is she ended up cheating on me. Yeah, she ended up cheating on me there, and that was going on there for a couple months towards the end of our relationship. I found out after-the-fact, and so she actually had cheated on me with another girl. It was actually a sorority sister of hers. Yeah, and so that happened.

Not only did the men talk about the ways in which infidelity was grounded in disrespect and jealousy, they also shared openly about their own infidelity. When asked about the circumstances that led to his divorce, Adam, a 45-year-old divorced father of four, cited his inability to remain faithful:

Bottom line, infidelity. When I first got married and we moved away, really all I wanted to do was be with her. That was enough for me because that's all I really knew, but after about two or three years, I started noticing other women which eventually led up to me cheating on her and that was really the beginning of the end. I can't sit here and lie and say she did anything wrong.

Beyond being cheated on or being unfaithful themselves, one of the more interesting findings that came out of the interviews was that the threat of infidelity was ever present and would sometimes be floated as a possibility by others as a way to cast doubt onto the men's relationships or as an attempt to manipulate them. First, Josh, whose history involved having multiple simultaneous relationships, recalled frequently being asked by former girlfriends and other women about whether he was happy with his wife in the early days of his marriage. In recalling these encounters, he mentions being asked if he was married and having women respond, "I like married men" after he told them that he was indeed married. In another example, Terrell shares that some of his co-workers and regular clients (who he described as jealous of his relationship with his wife) at the barbershop where he worked joked about the prospects of his wife being unfaithful while he was out of town.

> I'm at the barber shop, and everybody knows I'm married. For instance, I say I'm going out of town. "Well, shoot. You know how many people going to be out there at your house?" It's like, why you would even think such a thing? Why would you even want that to happen? That's just pretty much jokes or whatever. As far as me, I look at it as, y'all would like for that to happen, because y'all would love for me to look bad. That's the way we are in this world today. People love seeing other people do bad, so I don't present myself as any shape, show, or fashion to where I'm looking weak. I've bowed down a couple times and made myself look weak, bite into it, then we arguing back and forth. As far as now, I was doing so much in the last year over there to where, can't nobody tell me about my wife and how wonderful she is to me, because I'm the only one that knows. The ones that always got something to say is the ones that I can see in their marriages, they don't got everything going on the way they would want it to go on. Some people get married for financial reasons or have been hurt earlier in their life by somebody else. Whereas me, I love my wife like I want to be loved. I couldn't see myself going out here doing anything to embarrass myself or embarrass her.

Recognizing the ever-present threat of infidelity and his high-profile status as a pastor of a medium sized congregation disproportionately populated by women, Chris, a 60-year-old father of three, talked about his efforts to regularly reassure his wife.

> I think faithfulness is very important to me. I definitely have to have a woman that I feel like I can trust. Of course, by faithful to me I mean that I'm her only man. I think we both have tried to be very faithful to each other. As a pastor, you know you're going to have women hitting on you and that kind of thing. You just have to always show your wife that she's first.

Next, Peter, a 35-year-old married father, grounds his fidelity in his interest in having a long-term marriage like his own father, however without having to overcome an affair along the way.

My parents are married and they've been married for years, close to 40. They've been married 40 years since this past July. It hasn't always been smooth sailing, but they stayed committed. A lot of the things in my life and why I'm faithful to my own wife is because I saw the infidelity of my father. I said that when I get married, I'm going to be a faithful husband. That's a choice I made as a young adult. I didn't get married till I was 30. I just had my 10 year wedding anniversary. I lived my life that I wanted to live first. I got married and I'm committed to my wife. I don't regret that. I tell people all the time, if I wanted to chase other women and live that lifestyle then I'd get a divorce. There's no need playing the games. I asked my wife to have the same attitude. That's me, I've never been a deceitful guy. Even when I was single, it was hard to juggle two women. That's me and who I am. I think that it just comes with the territory.

Like both Peter and Chris, some of the other men were able to stay faithful by employing a strategy featuring proactively resisting temptation or avoiding placing themselves in precarious situations. In some cases, such as with Chad, a 50-year-old remarried father of three, this meant being selective about the company he keeps and limiting how often he goes out.

So, my expectation is to live what I talk about and position myself to do that by avoiding temptation. And a part of that is surrounding myself with the right people and not with the wrong people. That's why I don't have a large circle of men around me. I spend 90 percent of my time at home when I'm not at work. So, if you're looking for me, you know where to find me, at home.

Here, Chad shares how he chooses to avoid temptation by restricting his opportunities to engage in nefarious behavior. Josh, who had a history of infidelity, on the other hand, takes a slightly different perspective on motivation for faithfulness. In his attempt to keep a friend from having an affair, he focuses on how his friend would be impacted if his spouse engaged in similar behavior.

A brother told me, he said man I've been married for about a year, what can I do to keep my marriage alive 'cause I'm thinking about stepping outside and fucking. I said just picture your woman . . . I said you love your woman? He said yeah. I said do you know that guy from Amistad, the big ole black dude that said give us free? You know the one with that 12 inch dick? Just picture her legs open with him fucking her while you're off doing whatever it is you're doing [laughing]. 'Cause I couldn't imagine nobody laying up with my wife so we gotta imagine if she did the same thing you did. You know, we play big and bad and we usually are the cheaters but when they cheat, we can't take it.

As can be seen from the quotes, faithfulness in relationships and marriage came up quite often in the men's interviews. In some cases, actual infidelity by either the men's partners or the men themselves negatively impacted their relationships. In other cases, the threat of infidelity was weaponized in an attempt to create insecurity as with Terrell, or to manipulate or serve as a deterrent in the case of Josh and his friend. In conjunction with discussions related to the level of faithfulness that existed within the men's relationships, they also shared how much of a role the media has in shaping their sexual experiences and perspectives.

## Sex and Influence of Media

Closely related to the discussions of sex and faithfulness were those invoking the media. To be specific, in explaining some of the reasons for the infidelity in their relationships and the broader impact of infidelity on black marriages and romantic relationships, the men discussed the role of media. Excerpts from several interviews indicated that many of the men felt that the media contributes to a culture that encourages casual sex and infidelity. These sentiments are best represented by excerpts from interviews with William and Adam. First, William shares that the media glorifies sex, money, and drugs and does little to promote marriage.

> I mean I don't know for sure right. I don't study this stuff like you do, but I think a lot of it has to do with the images that we see nowadays. Like everywhere you turn, if you see black men on tv and in the media they're talking about sex, money and drugs. Marriage is not even on the radar. It doesn't seem like it's something that is discussed in families, at least as much as it should be. In our communities, marriage doesn't have the standing that it used to, you know. It's not a priority the way it used to be.

Like William, Adam also talked about the influence of the media. In addition to discussing the large number of sexual messages bombarding consumers of media, Adam also connects the pervasiveness of these messages to the increased probability that they will contribute to infidelity.

> To be straight with you, I have to address my own past you know. Infidelity is a big issue that wrecks a lot of relationships. Now I'm not saying that other people make you do something that you don't want to do, but I think the media plays a big part in the infidelity too. Tv and radio is straight sex. Everything is sex, sex, sex. Man, there is so much temptation that if you if are at a place where you can fall weak, the messages are all over the place. I know because I work in that field, you know. By the time they hit you with so many messages, all you can think about is sex even if it's only at a subconscious level. Like if you're walking down the street and you see a woman and she's good looking, you can see her as a beautiful woman and there ain't nothing wrong with that. Women are

beautiful. But the way the media is, like you'll see that same lady and instead of just seeing her as a beautiful woman, you start to go down the road of sin and you see more than her as a beautiful woman, you see her as a sex object. You be looking at her breasts and you know what happens as soon as she walks by you you end up turning around to look at her ass. I'm just being real. Then since you focused on that, then you want to try her to see what's going on and then at that point, you're already cheating because of how you're thinking about her.

In sharing his story with us, Adam expresses that he is of the belief that the media contributes to infidelity in relationships by flooding the airwaves with messages about sex and sexuality. Interestingly, Adam is uniquely qualified to offer this perspective because he both works in the media and has been unfaithful in his past relationships. It also turned out that his beliefs were similar to many other men who we interviewed who also thought that the media's overemphasis on sex negatively impacted marriages and romantic relationships. In fact, many of the men referenced several of the movies and tv shows that were included in the review of popular culture representations of black men in chapter 1. As they invoked them, often the men would cite the actions and behaviors of various characters and discuss how either they or someone around them had been in situations similar to those of the mediated images they consumed on tv and film.

## Intimacy

Based on the ways in which black men's sexuality has been framed in previous research and portrayed in popular culture, discussions related to casual sex, faithfulness versus infidelity, and the influence of the media were to be expected. Therefore, perhaps the most interesting and unexpected finding that came out of the interviews was when the men discussed their interest in achieving a high level of intimacy with their partners that did not necessarily involve sex. Most often when this happened, the men shared their efforts to connect with their partners' *love language,* a reference to Chapman's (2010) bestselling relationship book, as a way to achieve intimacy. First, there was Dan who in reflecting on one of his previous interviews talked about how he had evolved over time, transitioning from prioritizing superficial things to now placing emphasis on achieving deeper, more substantive connections.

I don't remember exactly what I said [in previous interviews], but I know right now I'm 30, I'll be 31 in June. Back then I was 25, 26, depending on when we did it, and I definitely know who I am now is different than who I was then. Expectation-wise, it was more of the superficial stuff then. Like, all this about who's going to show up and be present, and look supportive and give this idea, or project this image. Now I'm at the point where I much less care about the physical stuff, the sex stuff, all that kind of stuff. It's more about who's in my corner. I expect support, and consistency, and honesty, and loyalty. That's it more than anything. Those are the biggies. Like, to speak each other's love language. To love me as I need to and want to be loved, not to love me the way that feels convenient for the way you want to love me and vice versa, you know.

Next, Chris discusses how becoming more familiar with love languages helped him to understand that his wife was not rejecting him when she did not want to have sex as often as he did. Moreover, he discusses how he came to the revelation that he could be intimate with her without having sex.

I would be out all day long, come home, I'd want to be physically affectionate and hold her and that kind of thing. I want to do that and she's just the opposite actually. That was very, very difficult for me because I would think she didn't love me because she didn't always want to be as physical as I wanted to be. Understanding the love language has helped me, mentally, to process that. Helped her understand that I wasn't being doggish. It's who I am. It helped me to understand that hers was quality time. I'm a big sports fan. I could sit there watching the game and she'd really want to talk with me, and I would not give her my undivided attention. But I needed to physically turn from the game, maybe in some instances turn off the game, and give her eye contact and sit there. Sometimes, to be honest with you, she'd wear me out just talking, talking, talking about whatever she wanted to talk about. It was very important for her love language for me to put down my sermon, put down papers I'm grading, whatever I was doing to give her that attention. Understanding what our love language was, helped us work through those things. It's not easy, but it helped me mentally and her mentally to mentally and emotionally deal with that. I guess I had to lower my expectations in the physical touch area. If I would look back over my life, I would've wanted a much more sensual, sexy woman, although my wife is very appealing to me and all of that. I would have wanted more physical affection. I had to adjust my expectations to realize, I did not marry that woman who wants to make love three times a day. That's not my wife. I love her for so many other things that I can make some adjustment to that because some of that was my own selfishness.

Later Chris was able to explain that some of his newfound understanding and appreciation for intimacy came as a result of some of his experiences in pastoral counseling and seeing how other couples were struggling in their relationships and marriages.

I'm facing guys who are becoming impotent. They physically are impotent, diabetes, all this kind of stuff. If they don't have a healthy relationship with their wife, man, that marriage gets in trouble and they've been married for years. If you have a good relationship, you can find out that you can be intimate without having sex. If you don't have the foundation for that . . . man you in trouble!

Nick, a 43-year-old father of two, expressed a similar sentiment as he stated:

I think it's a mistake a lot of people make when they get married, or even if they're not married, but when they just hook up with somebody and not being on the same page. You caught up into other stuff and not really think through what it is you need to be connected on, especially when it comes to marriage.

In the passage below, Keith, a 27-year-old married father, speaks to the ways in which achieving intimacy with his now wife was the thing that motivated him to want to take their relationship to the next level.

I knew I wasn't going anywhere. You know you can have all the side females as you want. You can mess with females over here and broads over there, females here and there, but when you come home to that one and the others don't make you feel that way, you know you ain't going nowhere. Then let's say you were out there messin' with females here and there, but you always told them that I'm not leaving my girl and after a while, you get to a point where you just know. Dudes are more prone to go out there and do what they do than girls are, I guess that's how we're wired . . . I don't know, who knows. I guess when I got to that point where no other female was making me you know, feel the way I felt for her, that's what it was.

In discussing how the woman who became his wife made him feel and how that feeling was different than the feeling he got from other women he dated, Keith references the special connection that they shared. He also frames it using gendered stereotypes about what he believes to be men's and women's *wiring*. Nevertheless, he and others unveiled a perspective that was previously unrepresented or underreported in research on black men and their sexual attitudes and behaviors, that many of them seek, desire, and prioritize affection and intimacy (Mitchell 2007; Randolph 2018) that does not have to be accompanied by sex. Finally, we have Adam, who like Keith begins with a stereotypical men are from Mars, women are from Venus style trope on sex and intimacy, only to concede that many men, including himself, desire companionship and intimacy in their relationships.

That's what I would think about. Really got into something serious at my age right now, more than likely I would want to be . . . I don't know. Maybe I would have to consider that for sure before it got serious because . . . I would be dating women in their 40s probably soon. I already know going into it, our age bracket's that, that marriage is definitely on their mind, more than likely. Once in a while you find a couple that they're looking for companionship. They don't even have to be sexual, anything like that. They're just looking for companionship. That's just to get this started. I always thought if this is their nature to want to be with somebody, it's easier more so for them. Men like it, too. We want to be with somebody, too.

## CONCLUSION

In interviewing the men about their experiences and perspectives related to marriage and romantic relationships, sex and its role in shaping those experiences emerged as a salient factor. In the past, media, literature, and social science have all been used in intentional efforts to typecast black men as aggressive and even dangerously hypersexual. In more contemporary contexts, much of the extant research on black male-female relationships suggests men's preferred gender expression is characterized by bravado and posturing in what Majors and Billson (1992) referred to as the cool-pose and what Kniffley, Brown, and Davis (2018) have called compulsory masculinity. In some ways, the men's narratives were consistent with the existing research literature. This was true in the cases of Tim as he lamented his casual sex partners catching feelings or Adam who reported that the objectification of women in the media (Gammage 2015) contributed to his infidelity. Moreover, both Josh and Sean discussed how before they got married, they each juggled multiple relationships and were able to reconcile and rationalize them because they never lied about the additional relationships.

Yet, in other ways, the men's narratives took a divergent path from the stories told in research about black men. For example, contrary to Josh and Sean, Jeff talked about urging men to be not only honest, but also genuine about their intentions with their partners and potential partners based on a knowledge that many women desired more exclusive relationships than they initially agreed to or that these women might develop feelings as their relationships evolved. It was also true that several of the men openly discussed their desire for intimacy that was independent of sex. Most notably were Dan and Chris who shared that they worked to identify, understand, and connect to their partners' love language in order to achieve a higher level of intimacy. In doing so, these men offer an important counternarrative to shed light on the ways black men are examined in research. Thus, creating space for black men to share their perspectives in their own voices which has the potential to bring balance to disproportionately deficit framed literature and be particularly informative to future research.

# Chapter Four

# Trials, Tribulations, and Trauma

## with Azaliah Israel

"Trauma events call into question basic human relationships. They breach the attachment of family, friendship, love, and community. They shatter the construction of the self that is formed and sustained in relation to others" (Herman 1992, p. 51). In recent years, research on trauma and its effects has become an increasingly popular field of inquiry. Much of the interest in trauma began with the Adverse Childhood Experiences (ACEs) study. The ACEs study explored the relationship between risky health behavior and disease during adulthood and the extent to which abuse and household dysfunction was experienced during childhood. A total of 13,494 adults completed the ACE questionnaire which measured seven categories of trauma including psychological, physical, or sexual abuse; violence against one's mother; and living with household members who were substance abusers, mentally ill or suicidal, or ever imprisoned. The results revealed that there was a strong correlation between the level of abuse and dysfunction experienced during childhood and risky behavior and disease during adulthood (Felitti et al. 1998). Although trauma is a burgeoning area of inquiry, there is very little research on the ways in which it impacts black men and boys.

Interestingly, the source of trauma may not lie completely within the individual experiencing it but could involve direct or indirect generational transmissions of trauma. We borrow a second definition of trauma from Dr. Joy Degruy (2005) that embodies a more culturally relevant explanation of how trauma operates for the descendants of chattel slaves in America:

> Trauma is an injury caused by an outside, usually violent forwent, event or experience. We can experience this injury physically, emotionally, psychologically, and/or spiritually. Traumas can upset our equilibrium and wellbeing.

If a trauma is severe enough, it can distort our attitudes and beliefs. Such distortions often result in dysfunctional behaviors, which can in turn produce unwanted consequences. Recent research in the field of epigenetic has revealed that trauma can actually impact an individual's DNA, and the manifesto of the traumas experienced by prior generations can be passed along genetically to future offspring.

Degruy's primary thesis acknowledges the linkages between the behavioral patterns of black slaves who lived under the constant threat of violence and death throughout the 17th and 18th century U.S. and their descendants who never actually experienced these traumatic events in a physical sense. Post traumatic slave syndrome (PTSS) is a condition that persists for modern day black people developed as a result of undiagnosed physical, psychological, and spiritual trauma experienced by their ancestors. While physical torture and mutilations served to traumatize those of the past, the primary vehicle through which it operates today is racism. A discussion on black trauma absent of this important literature would be incomplete as it has warranted much respect within our communities by giving voice to the thought and behavioral patterns that many identify with but may not have been able to fully explain until now. Terms such as "vacant esteem" provide the necessary language in explaining the extreme sense of hopelessness and high levels of anxiety experienced by many in the black community today. As you will read in this chapter, the men referenced PTSS throughout the interviews in explaining their own behavioral patterns. To the extent that trauma has been explored with regard to black boys and men, it has been heavily concentrated on the effects of community violence or interactions with law enforcement and the criminal justice system.

## Community Violence

With regard to trauma affecting black men and boys, perhaps the most often researched area is community violence. In most cases, these studies examine the impact of living in socially and economically dislocated urban neighborhoods where residents are more likely to witness or be victims of violence. In a study aimed at better understanding the relationship between black adolescents' exposure to trauma, Jenkins, Wang, and Turner (2009), found that 69 percent of the 403 study participants had already experienced personal victimization by the time they reached the 8th grade and many others had witnessed life threatening events. The results also revealed that black boys experienced more trauma than black girls, they were more likely to exhibit internalizing and externalizing behaviors, and were more negatively affected by losing a friend or family member to violence than black girls. Similarly, in their study of 18- to 30-year-old black men who had been hospitalized after being shot, stabbed, or assaulted, Rich and Grey (2005) found that 65 percent of the study's sample meet the clinical criteria for post traumatic stress disorder (PTSD). They also concluded that emotional numbing was a consistent theme in how the men responded to trauma, as well as turning to substance abuse to truncate the effects of the trauma. Most recently, Hawkins (2017) reviewed the evaluations of programs providing services to survivors of community violence and unfortunately, found very few programs that were effective in addressing the needs of black men who had experienced violence in a community setting.

## Law Enforcement and the Criminal Justice System

In addition to black men being traumatized by community violence, research also indicates that their interactions with law enforcement and the criminal justice system also have deleterious effects on their functioning. Staggers-Hakim (2016) utilized a focus group methodology with black boys ages 14–18 to explore their perspectives on how police brutality impacted their overall mental health and social development. The themes that emerged from the focus groups were that black males are seen as a threat by society, the police should be feared, and that police killings can happen to any black male at any time. The black males in this study expressed that the desired outcome of interacting with law enforcement officers was to simply get home alive. In another study exploring black men's experiences and responses to police involved killings, Brooms and Perry (2016) found that study participants expressed feeling hurt, saddened, and frustrated, but were not surprised in hearing about the deaths of Mike Brown, Oscar Grant, Eric Garner, and others because according to them, it could be any black man, including themselves. The study's findings also revealed that because the participants knew that they were perceived as dangerous and as threats, they employed several strategies to mitigate risk, some of which included restricting their own movements and taking strides aimed at helping others see them as humans. Finally, there is Aymer's (2016) case study analysis of a young black man who was sent to therapy by his parents due to their concerns about his grades slipping. On his way to the first session, the young man was stopped, frisked, and detained by the police. The effects of the experience were so traumatic that they led to his refusal to attend the subsequent sessions for fear that he would be stopped and detained again.

Despite what we have learned about the impact of community violence and interactions with law enforcement and the criminal justice system, much less is known about how black men's romantic relationships are impacted by the trauma that they experience. In fact, although we know that trauma does influence relationship trajectories (Chung and Hunt 2013), other than Kogan,

Yu, and Brown's (2016) study concluding that the combination of black boys experiencing socioeconomic disadvantage, harsh parenting, and racism was associated with their difficulty in regulating their emotions and committing to their romantic relationships as men, scholars have openly acknowledged that black men are underrepresented in this research (Busby, Walker, and Holman 2011; Owen, Quirk, and Mathos 2012). Therefore, giving voice to how the men in our study reported that they and their relationships were impacted by their traumatic experiences represents a unique contribution to the state of knowledge related to black men and boys.

## Intimate Partner Violence

Intimate partner violence is used to describe acts of violence that occur within the intimate relationships of couples. Of all racial and gendered groups, the Centers for Disease Control (CDC) reports that black women are more likely to be victims of intimate partner violence (Petrosky et al. 2017). By comparison, we know very little about the ways in which their counterparts may experience violence in intimate relationships. The National Coalition Against Domestic Violence (NCADV) (2015) reports that 1 in 4 men have experienced physical abuse in the form of slapping, pushing, and shoving by an intimate partner. In regard to severe physical abuse like being hit with a fist and/or hard objects, kicked, slammed against something, choked, or burned, it decreases to 1 in 7 men. Almost 50% of men have experienced psychological abuse and stalking. West (2008) conducted a systematic review of the research literature to determine how black men participate in intimate partner violence as perpetrators but also as victims. The results of the review revealed that in one study, 64 percent of black male students reported being victims of physical abuse by a girlfriend. In another study, 50 percent of black male college students reported that they had been pressured to have sexual intercourse. West (2008) also concluded that overall, black men's experiences with victimization had been significantly neglected in the research literature. Therefore, the stories about the impact of the men's trauma on their romantic relationships and marriages shared in this chapter serve to fill a gap in the existing literature.

## BLACK MALE TRAUMA AND ROMANTIC RELATIONSHIPS

Recent research estimates that more than 60 percent of black males have experienced some trauma in their lifetime (Motley and Banks 2018). However, there is scant literature examining the ways in which black men and their relationships are affected by trauma. Therefore, we were not expecting it to be a focal point of the men's narratives. However, in telling their stories, nearly all of the men we interviewed reported that some form of trauma had impacted their attitudes or behavior in their marriages or romantic relationships. In operationalizing trauma, rather than relying on any formalized diagnoses, we subscribed to Lee's (2016) definition which described trauma as an experience or situation that 1) was emotionally painful or distressing; 2) overwhelms an individual's ability to cope, producing a sense of powerlessness; and 3) has lasting adverse effects on the individual's functioning and physical, social, emotional, or spiritual well-being. Using this definition as a backdrop, we found that with regard to prevalence, 32 of the 33 (96.96%) men reported that their relationships had been impacted by some form of real or perceived trauma. Given the near universal prevalence of some form of trauma, exploring their experiences piqued our curiosity. Moreover, the salience with which the men described these experiences and their impact, highlighting and uplifting them became paramount. To do so, the traumas reported in the men's narratives were grouped into three broad categories including psychological trauma, physical trauma, and relationship trauma.

## Psychological Trauma

The first of the three trauma categories was psychological trauma. These traumas included the fallout from direct and indirect exposure to mental illness, substance abuse, interaction with the criminal justice system, and emotional stress and how they impacted the men's relationship experiences and perspectives. In all, 13 of the 33 (39.39%) men reported that their relationships had been negatively impacted by these traumas.

Interestingly, many of the men invoked the lasting legacy of slavery as a psychological trauma negatively impacting their own relationships, as well as the relationships of large numbers of black men. In these instances, the men talked about how the peculiar institution restricted black men's authority in their relationships and kept them from fulfilling the same socially prescribed gender roles as their white counterparts. In other words, the men expressing this sentiment felt as though black men have never been allowed to assume their roles as providers and protectors. Since black men were not allowed to fulfill these roles during slavery, many of the men believed that the emasculation of black men has been woven into the fabric of black male-female relationships to the point where many contemporary black men find great difficulty assuming the role as the unquestioned heads of their households. John speaks to this as he elaborates on his thoughts related to obstacles facing black male-female relationships.

Slavery. I think that's one of the ones that had the biggest impact on us as a people. Otherwise, I'm not sure how to explain that. I think that separation of family and being sold off in different directions and the way the black male was treated in front of his family was kind of . . . it set a pattern of separation, the male feeling like he's not good enough to take care of the family and women feeling like they have to take care of the family on their own without the man. All of that has worked against us.

In this quote, John shares his thoughts on how historical traumas still have contemporary implications. Somewhat related, but beyond the specific impact of slavery, the men also talked about the psychological impact of being regularly confronted with statistics and demographic data reporting on how black families have disproportionately high rates of non-marital child births, divorce, and single female headed households. In an excerpt from an interview with Robert, an unemployed 29-year-old married father of three, he laments the lack of marital and familial role models for black men. Further, he believes that this absence of role models means that many black men never learn to comport themselves in a manner that will facilitate positive, sustainable relationships.

I've heard the statistics about how long black men tend to stay with their wives and all that and the divorce rates, but I don't know because we are all different, but I think it would stem from the way a lot of black men and women are brought up. We're talking single parent homes and rough environments you know. There was never no foundation set for them as far as what it takes for a man and woman to be together. You know I have family members and friends who grew up without a father or a father figure in the household and if they only grew up with their mom and never knew the dad then they didn't see how men supposed to treat women and how women supposed to treat men. Then they grow and get into they own relationships and they don't know how to cope with it, they don't know how to love and be a companion and stuff like that and the true meaning of intimacy and things of that nature. Not to say that's the case for all young black males and females, but there a lot in that situation. Enough to where they're not the exception, they're the rule, you know.

Apart from the injurious legacy of slavery and the contemporary impact of demographic challenges affecting black families, the men also talked about the ways in which other emotional stressors influenced their relationships. Two of the best illustrations were Brian and Terrell. Brian, a 31-year-old married father discussed the emotional toll that being a police officer takes on his relationship. In his initial interview, Brian talked about how regularly being exposed to other people's trauma made him emotionally numb and the negative implications for this marriage.

[Sighing] You know as far as cops go, we're mostly assholes. Two, it's kind of a hard profession to deal with for the other person, the spouse because we're always gone, we work late hours and it's just a life that you can never get used to. From what I'm told, lawyers and cops have the highest divorce rates . . . I can say I'm de-sensitized to a lot of things because of my job. I've seen so much that a lot of things don't bother me. Example, I could see a dead body and just be like, man hell what we gonna eat? It's just me going about my business. It could be a million people crying and I'm just sitting there like . . . yeah de-sensitized.

In discussing how his job has de-sensitized him to the pain and suffering of others, Brian also discussed how his inability to compartmentalize the trauma that he absorbs at work has rendered him emotionally unavailable in his personal relationships. In a follow up interview, Brian expands on this point and expresses some concern about the impact of his trauma exposure and the long-term viability of his marriage.

I'll say that it [being a police officer] still definitely stresses on the relationship. Like with anything, when you're gone a long time . . . the stress of dealing with what I do. Sometimes you try not to bring it home but sometimes it does follow you. That's one thing definitely that I've noticed more. Even now I caught myself, sometimes I'm really withdrawn because I'm thinking about things at work or I'm always working and things like that. Funny thing is . . . I'll say a lot of my cop friends, which happens naturally for police, you tend to eventually start hanging with more cops. Cops who are notorious to have bad relationships or be on your second and third marriage or just not be with anyone.

Added to the traditional stress and strain associated with being exposed to others' suffering, Brian goes on to explain how recent incidents like police involved shootings complicate and exacerbate the psychological stress impacting his marriage. What's interesting here is that in most contexts, any discussion of law enforcement, trauma, and black males revolves around the ways in which stereotyping, profiling, and police brutality impact black men. However, in this this case, the intersectional identities of Brian being both a black man and a police officer place him a very precarious situation that only serves to add to the stress and strain of an already emotionally draining job that negatively impacts his home life and marital relationship.

Then on top of all that, definitely with the way the general culture views the police officer. We're demonized pretty much. That plays a part too. Where it used to be one of the most . . . it's a proud job and this and that, but now it's kind of like you don't even want to let anyone know what you do. That plays a little part. Things like that, definitely. Oh yes, definitely. That's played . . . basically those two cases, especially the Michael Brown case, I'll speak on it. . . . Being a black police officer, you had the general black population that feels "Oh, you should be on our side." They don't like us anyway. How I tell people it's like, "Are some people racist?" Yeah. Unfortunately, some of those people happen to be cops, but then again there's a racist person cooking your food. You don't know. Unfortunately, our sentiment was like the general black public doesn't like officers, they definitely don't like black officers and then if there's a white officer they don't like us either. I was like so, yes, the black officers, we're 100% caught in the middle. And it's true, all of that stuff follows you home.

Next, there's Terrell. In chapter 3, Terrell discussed being intentional about avoiding temptation and honoring his wife in the face of co-workers who he described as jealous to the point there they would attempt to manipulate him into believing that his wife was being unfaithful. In addition to having to navigate the treacherous minefield of jealous co-workers, Terrell and his wife also experienced fertility issues. To be more specific, Terrell and his wife had multiple miscarriages before their son was born. The following is an excerpt from our final interview with him in which he shares some of the history of difficulties he and his wife had and how these past traumas created a sense of anxiety that led them to hide the new pregnancy from family. This was until their son's birth had to be induced 3 months premature. As he retold the story, Terrell talked about how he and his wife wanted and needed support from family that they could not receive because they decided not to tell anyone of the pregnancy for fear of another miscarriage. In the following excerpt, Terrell talks about how their attempt to protect themselves from the trauma and grief of another miscarriage also created a lot stress and placed tremendous strains on the relationship.

> We went to the doctor on a Monday to do a check-up, and they said, you've lost a lot of fluid, and you need to go on and have this baby right now. We need to have it by in the morning. Right then, you got to get together. You think you're going to work the next day, you got to sit around and figure out, shoot, we going to be at the hospital for ain't no telling how long. We hadn't told anybody she was pregnant. I refused this time to have my wife having to hear all of this about, I'm going to have a baby on February 8th. Then the baby don't come, and then she's got to deal with people saying, I'm sorry. I'm sorry. I'm sorry. Which is great that you have the type of people that will comfort you, but it's another thing coming home and having to look at this woman every day when she's done lost a kid. . . . He came into the world as a difficulty. Me and my wife have always had difficulties with having a child. We lost 2 kids in the course of our 8 years being together. Over the last 2 or 3, he has come along. He came to the Earth 3 months before he was supposed to . . . He came in November 30th. He was supposed to come February or March. He was born 1 pound, 3 ounces. . . . When a kid is born 1 pound, 3 ounces, you're going to have to deal with both sides of the family. You're going to need all the encouragement you can get.

We was having to run back and forth to the hospital for 3 months straight, every day, making sure that this boy was going to turn out all right.

Although the history of miscarriages and the fallout from them was unique to Terrell and his family, his story was emblematic of over one-third of the men whose narratives included psychological trauma that impacted their relationships. However, psychological trauma was not the only type that the men found themselves confronting. There was also physical trauma and relationship trauma, both of which are addressed in the following sections.

## Physical Trauma

The second of the three broad trauma categories was trauma of a physical nature. Although it was invoked less frequently than the psychological traumas, to those who were impacted by it, the effects were no less harmful and long lasting. Eight of the 33 (24.24%) men reported that their relationships had been negatively impacted by previous or current physical trauma that they had either experienced or been exposed to. These traumas included physical abuse, exposure to domestic violence, and sexual assault.

Both Josh and Paul's stories included physical abuse that later manifested itself negatively in their relationships. Josh shared how in reflecting on his approach and behavior in relationships, he realized that the women from his past, who he mistreated, all had a striking resemblance to a former babysitter who physically abused him as a child.

I like short women, petite women, but as I analyzed that like L. Ron Hubbard and all that, going to the psyche, you know . . . the lady who abused me when I was younger comes up. She used to whoop me all the time because I was a bed wetter late in age. Her name was [perpetrator's name], light skinned, real short. So, I analyzed the Minister [Farrakhan] when he was on this subject, talking about himself. He is talking about the 95%. He is just talking. He isn't talking to me, but you analyze and it hits me. When I thought back, all these women was, it was like a criteria. Real petite and short. Then I would get 'em and dog 'em up. Am I getting [perpetrator] back for her . . . I didn't even realize it until I looked back it after the fact.

According to Josh, he was not cognizant of the connection between the appearance of his abuser and the women that he recruited into a life of prostitution at the time when it was happening. Instead, he mentions that this realization was thrust upon him much later in life as a part of his spiritual reflection. On the other hand, Paul was a little different. In his situation, his abuse occurred as an adult and was perpetrated by his girlfriend at the time who wanted to control him and took advantage of him after he became disabled following an accident.

> We had been together 6 years. She wouldn't let all of that go. Then I would get the brunt of it. I thought I could handle that, but it [physical abuse] just started becoming too much. Even after a while she wanted me trapped in the house. After I messed up my leg, that's how she kept me there. She wanted me to be trapped in the house and just do nothing. Just like when a man can batter a woman and they don't want them to leave the house. She wanted to isolate [me]. She didn't want me to have a life. If I just want to sit outside and relax outside with the fellas and we all just sit and do what men do. You know, talk crazy about stuff. Sports or whatever. She was unhappy with that and that's how it started.

When asked about how he has been affected by the abuse, Paul responded:

> Actually, I think, that's one of the things I changed about myself. I'm not as sensitive now. That's one thing I can say. Dealing with women, I'm not as sensitive. I'm not as affectionate. I think it can hurt because I might just be non-affectionate to the person I'm actually with who needs that. I look at it as a flaw. I lost myself a little bit with that.

In recounting the impact of being abused by his girlfriend, Paul discusses how he became less sensitive and affectionate toward his subsequent partners. As we learn in chapter 5, Paul had several relationships in the period of time during the study, a few of which progressed to the point of marriage proposals. However, they each lacked the necessary intimacy and commitment to be sustainable in large part owing to emotional withdrawal and detachment that came about as a result of the abuse he suffered.

Dan also suffered abuse that had long lasting effects. However, in his case, he was sexually abused as a child. As he explains, his assault led to feelings of shame and depression. Dan's assault also contributed to uncertainty and questions related to his sexuality. As he shares in chapter 6, these unresolved questions along with social pressure from his family compelled Dan to pursue fraudulent heterosexual relationships in an attempt to avoid the shame and ridicule that he felt would come his way if any of his friends or family found out he was gay.

> Specifically, what happened was I was struggling with my sexuality. I was sexually assaulted when I was eight years old at a basketball camp, raped by one of my counselors. I never talked about it for years and years and years, never told anybody for years and years and years. Depressed, you know what I'm saying? You know how black people are. Not just black people, but people in general, certain stuff you just don't talk about. Certain stuff, you just don't deal with, so

I never even went there. Through college and all of this other stuff, depressed, depressed, depressed, and then it was kind of like, "Okay, I need to deal with this," so I started going to counseling, started doing all this kind of stuff. . . . Culturally for years I have learned and been taught and been conditioned to never put my masculinity into question, whether it's the right or wrong. That masculinity is sacred and to say, okay, I might be gay, I might not be 100% straight, I might be bisexual. But in my culture, in my upbringing, in my background, that is not man.

Dan continued to struggle internally until he came to the realization that he was indeed gay. Unfortunately, at the time, he was involved in a serious committed relationship with a woman. Dan explains how rather than being transparent with his girlfriend about his sexuality, he instead chose to treat her badly attempting to drive her away.

Back on the floor in my house it was like, here are the reasons to marry her, and I didn't list them. I thought about it, here are the reasons to marry her, here are the reasons not to marry her. Do you really want to marry this girl? Is that fair to her if you bust up or, you know, there's some shit that you need to deal with, and I was like no. I wanted to tell her, but, again, black man, cool guy, pastor, you can't go there, so the bitch move is what I did. Okay, I'm not going to break up with her. I want her to do it, so somehow, I thought being an asshole and making her breakup with me was better.

Slightly different from the other men, Quincy was not a victim of physical abuse. Rather, he was exposed to his mother's victimization. In his situation, the divorced 37-year-old father and community organizer, shared an experience where he witnessed domestic violence between his father and mother:

I'll tell you a quick story about my mother and father. It was actually my mother who taught me that domestic violence doesn't work. She said that . . . she was 4 months pregnant and my father decided that she needed to do something and she explained to him that she just wasn't gonna do it and he backhanded her. Then he looked at her and told her that I did that to let you know that I can do that whenever I get ready to. And she said ok . . . so later she fixed dinner, they ate and then he went to sleep so she went in the kitchen and got a butcher knife, sat on his chest, put the knife to his neck and told him that I just want to let you know that I can do this whenever I wanted to. She said after that, the arguments were a lot different. Obviously, that was the start of the downfall of their relationship. So that's why I never get into domestic violence and I have respect for women 'cause I tend to see my mother as the ideal woman so I know what she's capable of so I'll never put my hands on a woman because I know what she's capable of. But anyway, back to the mindset . . . we have to first start by not being so selfish and get to the point where when we get into a relationship, you're really committed to it . . . not to the point of no matter what happens but to the point where there are breaking points and it should be something that is established in the beginning you know . . . I'm not gonna stay with you if you put your hands on me, I'm not gonna stay with you if you do this or that. Now that's not to give the other person leeway to do whatever they want as long as they don't cross the line, it's just to set up boundaries up front.

Although Quincy talked to us about how witnessing this abuse taught him that domestic violence is never an appropriate response to conflict, he also shared with us how sensitive he is to believing that his partners were attempting to control him. This perceived controlling behavior manifested itself in several ways including Quincy believing that some of his partners had secretly conspired to "speed up his timeline" regarding the seriousness of the relationship. In other words, on multiple occasions, Quincy broke up with previous girlfriends when they became too assertive for his liking in their attempts to engage him in discussions related to the prospects of cohabiting or marriage. In several cases, Quincy admitted that these were indeed mere conversations that would otherwise seem like the natural progression of a romantic relationship that had been going on for an extended period of time. However, because of his skepticism and belief that the women were trying to control him, Quincy's interpretation of these conversations was that the intent behind them was less than pure.

### Relationship Trauma

While it is certainly the case that all of the traumatic events experienced by the men had deleterious effects, their stories indicated that both the most frequent and most damaging form of trauma was that which emanated from early relationships or the impact of significant others' previous relationships. In fact, 23 of the 33 (69.69%) men reported that their relationships had been negatively impacted by relationship trauma. These traumas included impactful negative previous relationship experiences including infidelity, high conflict relationships, and the relationship inhibiting perspectives and behaviors of the men's families of origin. Ultimately, the effects of these traumas contributed to an inability or unwillingness to trust for several of the men.

One of the more traumatic relationship experiences reported by the men we interviewed was being cheated on by a former romantic partner. In most cases, the infidelity led directly to the end of the romantic relationship. However, the effects of these experiences continued well after the relationship dissolved. In Josh's experience, it was witnessing a former girlfriend take advantage of men's generosity that contributed to his decision to begin manipulating and exploiting his romantic partners.

I've watched women dogging men, you know, back when I was out there. I would have money . . . I had a girlfriend then, take her shopping, and I get over there and she say, hey it's a nigga that dropped off $100, let's go buy something. I'm thinking like, I was on my way to go buy you something. And I watched how women viewed men. So, from then until now, that's where the doggedness came up.

Here, Josh opens up about the origins of his "doggedness." To be more specific, he was so impacted by the combination of this infidelity and the physical abuse he suffered at the hands of a childhood babysitter that he set out to exploit women rather than be taken advantage of by them. This behavior became so extreme that for a period of time, he became a pimp with a steady group of between five to seven women who prostituted themselves for his financial benefit.

## High Conflict Relationships

In addition to dealing with the fallout from infidelity, many of the men's relationships suffered from being chronically high conflict in nature. Contrary to the shock and awe of learning of a partner's unfaithfulness, the trauma associated with having been in a high conflict relationship also proved to be injurious to the men's relationship trajectories. Emblematic of this was Anthony, a single 19-year-old college student, who experienced multiple break-ups between interviews. In describing the impact of these breakups and the circumstances leading to them, he mentions his former partner's propensity for "flipping" on him which led him to end the relationship.

I've actually been in a long-term relationship, 6 month relationship since then, and that didn't turn out well. The person completely flipped on me. One of the dumb arguments we had was she wanted me to put bleach in the soap. We had been together for 6 months, I have never washed dishes in bleach. She just went off about there being no bleach inside the dishwasher. Stuff like that to the point oh, and I guess one of the deeper ones was the way she wanted to react to her son. Her son is not my son. Originally, she was like, treat him like he's your child, stuff like that. At one point I told him to stop talking to his grandmother in a certain way, because respect your elders. She was like, that's her job to do it, not my job to do. . . . You know black women, they get their little finger shake and all of that when they start talking, I don't deal with that. I don't deal with any aggressive behavior. Like I said, my girlfriend before her, she laid her hands on me. At that point, I just walked out. That was the end of the relationship. I ain't giving no other chances or nothing.

Anthony ends his quote by stating that after his breakup with a woman who "flipped" on him, he "ain't giving no other chances." This notion of being unwilling to work toward reconciliation was a popular refrain. For many of the men, the constant tension of being engaged in a high conflict relationship and pain associated with finally ending the relationship proved to be so draining that they rendered themselves emotionally unavailable for any make up possibility. Going a step beyond Anthony, Paul professed an aversion to engaging in any level of relationship with his ex-girlfriend with whom he shared a child.

> If you're in the past, you're in the past. I don't want to be your best friend. If we couldn't work out as a couple, why we need to be friends. I'm not friends with my baby's mother. I love my son, but I'm not her friend. As a person, I don't like her, I ain't gonna lie. I told the mother of my son that I don't ever want to talk to you unless something is wrong with my son, he is hurt, or if he is acting a fool in school, we have nothing else to discuss. [Laughing] I don't wanna just be around a woman arguing all day.

Finally, there's Michael. When we first met Michael, he was a 61-year-old divorcee. In sharing his story, he talked candidly about the fact that never fully recovered after his marriage ended in his 20s. As Michael explained, the events leading up to his divorce were the things that made the divorce so difficult and traumatic. He shared that seemingly out of nowhere, his wife left him and took their daughter. He mentioned that he had no idea where his daughter was and had no contact with her for months until he was summoned to court for a child support hearing.

> I was hurt, I was angry. I was bitter for a while, but I found out you can't . . . There's a saying that you just have to let go and it's rough and it hurts, but you have to let go. I would tell anyone don't carry a grudge, just move. . . . Life goes on and uh, it was rough for a while 'cause I couldn't see my daughter for a while and then with her [the ex-wife], she told me don't come visit her and I didn't know where my daughter was. I think she was trying to hurt me. . . . Sometimes women will say things, but I know they know how to hurt a man. She played that one. You know, I got burned by getting married and I thought it was the right thing to do because I had a child and I loved her, I admit that. I think that's the part that hurt me the most when she left.

As he reflected on the effects of his divorce, Michael admitted to being confused, angry and bitter. Eventually, after reconnecting with his daughter, Michael said that he got to a place where he was able to let his bitterness go. However, more than 30 years later, he admitted that in addition to never remarrying, he also never had any romantic relationships serious enough to give strong consideration to marriage.

## Family of Origin Issues

The final form of relationship trauma that the men discussed was that which came in the form of exposure to the negative perceptions or experiences of

family members. In these cases, the men talked about hearing negative com-
ments and conversations, as well as seeing the struggles of their relatives
which served to quash their interest and willingness to engage or commit to
romantic relationships or marriage. First, there's Alex, a single 18-year-old
student who at a very early age received negative messages about the nature
of male-female romantic relationships.

> I grew up listening to my aunt tell my cousin that you gotta get a man with
> money, so now you've already put the relationship in a certain context and when
> it falls short of that, then it's a problem or it's not a good relationship. But that's
> not what a relationship is about. It's about co-existing and getting to know each
> other and if you already have a pre-conceived notion about what the relationship
> should be based on and it fall short, it's a problem. Then, where is the affection?
> Now I'm not talking about lust, I'm talking about affection and I don't see a lot
> of affection in our relationships.

In his quote, Alex is able to recall his aunt teaching her children to prioritize
money over emotional connection, affection, and partnership. In doing so, he
says that she was helping to create an expectation for what truly matters in relationships. Although Alex felt this expectation and emphasis on money was
misguided, the fact that it was espoused by his own aunt led him to believe
that others were being receiving similar, albeit misguided messages. What
was most problematic for Alex was that in his estimation, the fact that large
numbers of people being taught that money was the most important thing in
relationships was at the root of many of the troubles between black men and
women and their marriages or romantic relationships.

Next is Anthony in his initial interview explaining his reaction to being
asked if he thought he would ever get married.

> Right now, marriage is a joke. Marriage is a legal agreement 'cause my dad has
> been married for 15 years to my stepmom and they have been through rough
> times, but they don't communicate. My dad has cheated a couple times and it's
> like I don't see any real cooperation and it's like the only reason they're still
> together is because they got kids.

Anthony makes it clear that marriage is not on his radar and does not believe
it is in his future based largely on the model set for him by his father who he
knows has been unfaithful on multiple occasions. This leads him to conclude
that the presence of the children is the only thing buttressing his father and
stepmother's marriage. Therefore, he sees marriage as nothing more than a
"legal agreement." Not only were fathers instrumental in shaping the men's
attitudes and beliefs, so too were mothers. In fact, in discussions centering
on the family of origin and its influence, mothers were invoked more often

than fathers. For example, Amir talks about the ways in which his mother's influence had direct implications for one of his past relationships, ultimately leading to its dissolution.

> I also treated women different when my relationship with my mother was different. That's something I can confess to. Well me and my mother had a great relationship until I fell in love with a girl and I was faithful to her. Everything was going good, but my mother didn't like the relationship so we ended up getting into it.

Notable here is Amir's admission of faithfulness to this particular girlfriend. In mentioning it, he placed emphasis on the fact that at the time, exclusivity was something that all of his girlfriends expected, but very few received. Thus, the fact that he was faithful to this particular girlfriend was an indication that he had genuine feelings for her. Therefore, he was deeply saddened when he felt compelled to end the relationship because of his mother's disapproval.

Now consider Keith. Although the influence of Keith's mother was more indirect than Amir's, it was no less impactful. In sharing the circumstances surrounding him being separated from his wife at the time of his follow up interview, he talked about his mother and her role to his socialization around relationships.

> I'm nonchalant, I don't show a lot of passion. I don't show a lot of emotion. Just the way I grew up. My mother was hardcore. She was stern. My mother is from Brooklyn, New York and she's 100% New York bred. She showed no emotion in how she grew up in her household. My grandfather didn't show emotion. He was very hard, very direct so she raised me and my sister like that . . . I've always wanted to change in that sense. I had to just really tap into myself and realize that I'm that type of person. Back in 2011, when me and my wife split for seven months it opened my eyes for sure. I felt like I was providing financially for my family, but I wasn't providing that emotional touch that I needed.

In offering this quote, Keith recognizes the way that his mother's "hardcore" stance negatively influenced his relationships, including contributing to a separation from his wife. In looking to remedy the situation, he admits to falling short in the emotional expressiveness arena.

Finally, we have Jeff and William whose stories both speak to the long-range impact of being exposed to relationship troubles in the family of origin. Despite the fact that both Jeff and William eventually married (William divorced and remarried), from each of the excerpts below, it is clear that they both carried baggage resulting from their parents' failed marriages. In our first interview with Jeff, he shared that his mother had been married and divorced three times, compelling him to state, "whatever needed to be poured into me, wasn't" with regard to marriage and role modeling. As a result, even though he had a loving relationship with his new wife, he always felt uneasy, so he sought out constant reassurance because of his concern that something would go wrong. Below he describes this anxiety and what he needed from his wife:

> I was really needy, like consistent reassurance. That she wasn't going nowhere. That she was still invested. That I haven't screwed it up. Because I was taking so much risk. Again, not understanding what she really wanted out of the relationship. We didn't make what we made last year—right. I'm feeling like I'm not doing a very good job, so I need you to tell me that I'm doing a good job. Yeah. I need you to tell me that everything with you is going fine. There's still a little bit of that to this day. You look at it, the company started doing extremely well, but now it's in the silo and it's back. I'm the only this and the only that. I'm looking at her like, okay, you are feeling this, right?

Jeff's quote illustrates the trepidation he felt even after getting married based on the challenges that his mother experienced in staying married. Similarly, William was also negatively impacted by the relationships in his family of origin. In fact, William says that he was traumatized by his parents' divorce because of the ways in which it necessitated a change in the family's residence and financial status. In the following excerpt, William explained how these experiences followed him into adulthood and had a lasting effect on the way he viewed marriage and romantic relationships into the foreseeable future.

> I think my parents' divorce really impacted me. I flunked the third grade, I think primarily because I was so traumatized. In the year that they separated, I just kind of shut down in terms of my interactions with people. That stands out in my mind, and all the changes that resulted from it. We had to move to a different residence, went to different schools. Had to deal with financial issues that weren't there while they were married. Plus, other men coming into my mother's life. For a boy, that really impacts you, at least from my perspective it did.

## Trust

The ultimate result for many of the men whose experiences included infidelity, high conflict relationships, and being exposed to the negative experiences and perspectives of their family members was a decrease in their ability or willingness to trust their romantic partners. Given its central role in any relationship and romantic relationships in particular, the reduced level of trust posed a significant threat to the health of the men's current and future relationships. Offering insight into the ways in which trust issues impacted his relationship, Nick expressed reluctance to marry his longtime girlfriend in his initial interview, in large part because of trust issues developed from other relationships.

I'll tell you another thing, them still having baggage from old relationships. Whether it was something that happened to them in other relationships and then they thought I was going to be the same way. One girl I dated, hell every time her ex-boyfriend got in trouble she would be like, I gotta be there for him. No you don't. Why you gotta be there for him? So after a while, that got old and it wore out the relationship. It was like, we could have hung in there for about another year, but after all of that, I was like if you always gotta be there for this brother . . . go be with him. I ain't got time for that. It was just things like that, you know.

As Nick explains, his girlfriend's preoccupation with being available for her ex-boyfriend was a major point of contention that made it difficult for them to prioritize their relationship. As a consequence, no trust could be developed. Although he eventually did marry a subsequent girlfriend, the fact that they never fully developed the type of trust necessary to sustain a healthy marriage continued to plague their marriage, ultimately leading to a separation.

I think in the beginning for almost the first two years, there was still a lot of *I* going on. A lot of *I*, and she will agree with me when I say this, the *I* was on her part. I, my, this is my house, this is my stuff, I'm doing this. It was more so on her end. When we got married, to me, and to us, she still maintained her stuff, this is my opinion, this is my approach—that was a challenge in the beginning, a real big challenge, and trust, I think. She didn't trust me as much as she thought she would. Those things came into play and it led to us separating. But, I think once we separated, we didn't separate with the idea of, "Hey this is the end," it was more like, "Hey, let's pick stuff back up and try to figure out what's going on." Yeah, I think that those issues are what led up to the separation, because on my end I didn't trust her when it came to us making decisions. I thought she was—I was—making decisions that she thought was in her best interest and not in the best interest of the whole. She was still operating in terms of *I*. And you asked me this earlier, she was operating like she was before we got married, because she was a single mom and because she bought her house as a single woman, she was so used to doing everything on her own. It was hard for her to stop doing that, and it was a challenge.

Here, Nick explains that that from his perspective, there was a lot of selfishness on his wife's part that hindered their marriage in the first few years. They had both been single parents for quite some time and had established independent lives, so coming together and pooling resources like houses and finances became a challenge. This was particularly the case for Nick as he re-acted to his wife's use of the word *I* in referring to what he thought were *their* possessions. Like Nick, Thomas' marriage was fraught with trust issues that made sustainability difficult. However, unlike Nick, whose trust issues cre-ated a barrier to taking his relationship to the next level that he and his part-ner eventually hurdled (albeit temporarily until they separated), the mistrust in his Thomas' marriage led to a divorce where he subsequently adopted a stance of not even being willing to consider marrying again. Below, Thomas, a 47-year-old-graduate student and father of four, shares how the impact of his ex-wife not trusting him led him to not trust her, eventually leading to their divorce as he responds to being asked if he had considered remarrying.

> Not in the near future but I mean it is a possibility . . . maybe 7 to 10 years down the line, but right now, I wouldn't do it in the near future. Because of . . . because of what I had to deal with in my previous marriage. Ultimately, my integrity was being questioned and um . . . and then my leadership role within the relationship was being challenged and those are not things that I'm willing to compromise on. Um . . . [I want] a woman who I can trust. 'Cause ultimately if a person can't trust you, then they can't respect you.

As Thomas explains, the conflictual nature of his relationship with his ex-wife essentially soured him on the institution of marriage. Although he mentioned that he might be open to marriage, "7 to 10 years down the line," when we last interviewed him, Thomas disclosed that he was not dating, had not dated anyone in years, and was not looking for anyone to date. In sum, Nick and Thomas' feelings were representative of many of the men who had experiences that they described as traumatic for the ways that they made developing trust, a critical component in any romantic relationship, very difficult, if not impossible to establish and maintain.

## CONCLUSION

Nearly all of the men reported having experienced some form of trauma that had implications for the trajectory of their current or subsequent marriages or romantic relationships. These traumas were psychological, physical, and relational in nature. More specifically, these traumas included concerns about whether black men and women's relationships still suffer from the vestiges of slavery, contemporary race-based discrimination and oppression, work related stress, financial strain, unfaithful partners, discouraging relationship role models, physical abuse, sexual assault, and domestic violence. To be clear, despite the fact that all but one of the men reported their relationship trajectories were impacted by some form of trauma, not all of the men were equally impacted by the effects of their traumatic experiences. Some went on to have long term romantic relationships and even marriages or remarriages post trauma. Yet for others, the effects were much more devastating and longer lasting. When this was the case, the effects of these traumas were debilitating to say the least. In terms of how they were manifested, there was a great deal of variability. On one end of the spectrum, this would include men like Michael who stated that after his wife left him and kept him from seeing his daughter, "I was bitter, I didn't want to trust, I didn't want to get close to someone again, so I kept my friendship or relationships at a distance." On the other end of the spectrum, rather than disengaging from women and romantic relationships, men like Dan and Josh entered into romantic relationships under false pretenses. Dan did so as he sought to mask the effects of his previous sexual abuse and current struggle with his sexual orientation and Josh aimed to coerce women who resembled his abuser into prostitution and exploitation. Regardless of how severely and for how long the men were impacted, it remained that the most common result of these traumatic experiences was the negative impact on their interest and ability in establishing, cultivating, and maintaining the level of trust that would facilitate long lasting, positive, and supportive marriages or romantic relationships. In chapter 5, the sustainability of the men's relationships is explored through an examination of the number and type of relationship transitions that they experienced during the study period, as well as the circumstances surrounding those transitions.

## Chapter Five

# A Change Gonna Come

In sharing their relationship experiences over the 4-year study period, the men also chronicled their relationship transitions and the circumstances surrounding them. Learning more about the men's relationship transitions was interesting because most of the existing research in this area focuses on whether and for how long cohabiting couples get and stay married (Edin and Kefalas 2005; Vespa 2013) or how people are impacted by divorce or relationship instability (Anderson and Greene 2005; Barr et al. 2016; Dailey et al. 2013; Luciano and Orth 2017). These studies have found that couples who cohabit before marrying report more discord and lower marital quality than couples who did not cohabit before marrying (Halpern-Meekin and Tach 2013) and that black cohabitors are less likely to marry and more likely to remain cohabitors than whites (Rinellie and Brown 2010). Research has also concluded that people leaving or losing relationships tend to decrease their body mass index, but increase the odds of adopting unhealthy behaviors like smoking and alcohol consumption (Josefsson et al. 2018), and that individuals reporting multiple transitions consistently reported the poorest quality of life (Roberson et al. 2018). Moreover, these studies disproportionately examine women's experiences (Sassler, Michelmore, and Qian 2018). One such study was Lichter et al. (2006) investigation of relationship transitions among low income cohabiting women. Through an analysis of data from the National Longitudinal Survey of Youth, it was revealed that half of all cohabiting relationships ended by dissolution (not marriage) within one year and 90% ended by the end of the fifth year. The authors concluded that cohabitation is more likely for poor women than nonpoor women and is also more likely to be seen as a viable long term substitute for marriage. Brown (2000) analyzed National Survey of Families and Households data and concluded that women's negative assessments of their relationships were associated with increased odds for separation and that cohabitors' expectations that their relationship would dissolve was also associated with transitions out of the relationship. Monte-murro's (2014) examination revealed how marriage, separation, and divorce all served as integral turning points for women's sexuality such that the rela-tionship transition led some women to enhance their sexual confidence and assertiveness when it came to seeking pleasure, but inhibited other women's sexual agency and made them feel disconnected from their sexual selves.

Although small in relation to the number of studies on women's relation-ship transitions, there is an emerging literature on men's relationship transi-tions. The consensus of these studies is that being involved in a romantic relationship, particularly marriage, is generally good for men's well-being (Sitgraves 2008). For example, analyzing longitudinal data from more than 2,000 men and women, Chipperfield and Havens (2001) found men's life sat-isfaction declined more than women's after losing a spouse and their life sat-isfaction increased over time beyond that of women's life satisfaction if they gained a spouse over the 7 year study period. Haldane, Mincy, and Miller (2010) analyzed data from the Fragile Families and Child Well-being Study and found that men who transitioned to marriage 3 years after the birth of a child reported fewer serious health problems. The results from these studies support the notion that marriage and committed romantic relationships pro-vide men with a grounding that offers them a sense of comfort and familiarity with possible positive implications for their conceptualization of masculinity, a topic that is explored in chapter 6. Despite what we have learned from these studies examining men's relationship transitions, very little is known about the circumstances surrounding black men's relationship transitions, as well as how those relationships shape their relationship trajectories into the future.

Given the scant literature on black men's relationship transitions, the fac-tors contributing to them, and the ways in which they are impacted by them, there was interest in following the men over time to track their relationships, as well as the attitudes, philosophies, and experiences that shaped them. To do so, this chapter chronicles the trajectory of the men's relationships and their perspectives on the contributing circumstances. In inquiring into the men's relationship trajectories, the details of their original interviews were summarized, and they were asked to provide a general update including any changes in their relationship status. To elicit richer, more in-depth responses, subsequently the men were asked follow up questions about the factors con-tributing to the changes or stability of their relationships over the four-year study period. Thirty-two of the original 33 (97%) men completed the final follow up interviews. Unfortunately, Tim passed away two years before the final interviews were conducted. In defining their relationships, the men were asked to only focus on those that they considered to be serious, not women they dated casually. Transitions were defined as going from not being in a relationship to being in one, going from having a girlfriend to being married, going from either being married or having a girlfriend to getting divorced or being single, or being married and experiencing a separation. Of the 32 participants completing the final follow up interviews, 15 (47%) reported at least one relationship transition in the four-year study period. These transitions included three men going from not being involved in a romantic relationship to having a serious girlfriend, five men went from being divorced or single to being married, four men went from being involved in a romantic relationship to breaking up and remaining single, and three men were married but experienced a separation during the study period. Following are selected excerpts from interviews with the men experiencing each of the four types of relationship transitions during the study period. In addition to discussing the types of transitions, the men's perspectives on the circumstances surrounding the transitions are also presented.

## RELATIONSHIP TRANSITIONS

Over the 4-year study period, three of the men went from not being involved in any romantic relationship to having a girlfriend with whom they reported having a serious commitment. For these men, the follow up questions centered on inquiring into what, if anything had changed in their lives that led to them being more open to having a romantic relationship than they had been previously, how they met their current partner, and what was it about their new partner that attracted them. In two of the cases, originally, the men were adamantly against entering into a romantic relationship while the third man was more neutral and open to the possibility of entering into a new relationship. First, there was Anthony. Prior to meeting his current partner, Anthony explained that there was one other relationship transition during the study period. In response to how and why he decided to start dating again after a bad break up with this previous girlfriend who "flipped on him" for not putting bleach in the dishwasher, he shared that his relationship with his current girlfriend started out as a friendship grounded in intellectual curiosity, as well as self-reflection and discovery.

> Really, we just started talking and it was more intellectual things on some topics she was talking about on her [social media] page. We just started conversing. A month later we actually started going out. We learn from each other. It's just like a partnership. Not like we're both Christians, because I'm not. I'm an African spiritualist and she was asking questions about stuff like that. That's why our conversation started. She was just showing interest in it. She's still looking for

her path. It's still something that we have in common . . . I have been through a hell of a lot the past couple of years. And I just feel like I take people as they are. I've actually been in a long term relationship, 6 month relationship since then, and that didn't turn out well. The person completely flipped on me. The way I see it is, you've just got to roll the dice. You never know what somebody is. You never know how they're going to change. Either you roll the dice, or you won't be in a relationship.

That Anthony's relationship with his former girlfriend who flipped out on him did not last was not surprising because in his original interview, he stated, "most of the women I've been with, I argued with and I don't like to argue. Either you say what you got to say to me like an adult or don't talk to me." Similarly, Quincy also had some reservations about pursuing a romantic relationship during the initial interview. Prior to the start of the study, Quincy had been divorced and admitted that he probably married too young. Based largely on this experience, Quincy stated that he had dated causally, but had not entertained the idea of a serious, exclusive relationship for years due to his difficulty in establishing trust with potential partners. Some of this began to change when he met his current partner. Before meeting her, he shared that he was turned off by women who he felt made attempts to force him into a committed relationship before he was ready, with some going so far as to try to cohabit prematurely. Among other things, the fact that his current girlfriend respected his boundaries and gave him space to "do him" made her stand out as a viable option for a serious relationship. Quincy explains in his own words below.

Not really. I still believe that, for me personally, it takes a couple of years to get to the point where I'm at least ready to start thinking about marriage. Just because I'm slow about it. I have dated one or two different individuals who definitely had different expectations than I did. We dated a couple months and they would start talking about—how did she put it—one of the things was, she wanted to start sharing space. I was adamantly against that. It's not that she wanted to move in, it's just that she didn't want to leave. She'd come over on a Saturday at 2 o'clock, and at 9 o'clock, she'd still be there. I'm like, "cool." Monday morning, I'm like it's time to go. She's like, "I don't have to work today," and I'm like, "Okay, but you have an apartment." I had to break up. I like individuals who allow me to have insights and allow me to be independent. In my current relationship, we have a bunch of shared friends and we get together on a regular basis as a group, but sometimes I'm like, "I don't feel like it." And it's like, "All right, then. Peace," and she leaves. I appreciate that. Don't press me into doing something that I don't want to do.

Unlike Anthony and Quincy, John did not express strong feelings either for or against being in a romantic relationship in his initial interview. However, in his follow up interview, He shared that his current partner was an old friend and classmate with whom he worked early in his career. In addition to their occupational similarities, they were both divorced and had moved back to Louisville after having lived out of town for years.

> We both graduated from Manual [High School]. We worked on the school newspaper together. Worked the *Louisville Defender* together. Never dated at all during that time. She went to IU [Indiana University]. I went to Western Kentucky [University]. She married a guy there and moved to Virginia and came back in the last five years too, started to take care of her elderly parents. We ran into each other and she was divorced at that point. We ran into each other at a party.

In discussing what attracted him to her, John talked about their shared interests and the ease with which they seemed to get along. However, ironically, it was the way that his current partner resolved conflicts when they did not get along that made him interested in pursuing the romantic relationship. In the following quote, he describes the functional way in which he and his current partner are able to disagree without it lingering or turning into something more serious as a marker indicating the healthy nature of their relationship.

> We just express how we feel and we're over it. We move on. Nothing is that serious that it becomes a major point of, you know, people have to go to their separate corners and sit it out for a while. She talks about it and gets it out and she's done and then, of course, I'll go into my shell like a lot of guys do and don't talk about it. Before the end of the day she's gonna pull it out of me and get it over with. I just consider it to be a fairly healthy relationship. I think it's a relationship of equals. Nobody thinks they're better than the other person and nobody thinks they're better than anybody else outside the home. My ex-wife was uppity and judgmental.

Of the 15 men who reported experiencing at least one relationship transition during the study period, one-third of them went beyond going from being single to having a serious girlfriend. Rather, these men not only entered into committed, romantic relationships, but they also formalized those relationships by marrying. For two of these men, they eventually married the women that they were dating at the time of their initial interview while the other three men married women that they were not dating at the start of the study. Both Jeff and Reggie had girlfriends at the beginning of the study and in fact, Jeff was engaged. At the time, Jeff expressed a great deal of trepidation about the facts that his father was not active in his life and his mother had been married and divorced three times, leading him to believe that he did not have the capacity to be successful at marriage. Despite his concerns, Jeff and his fiancé married as planned. According to Jeff, he and his wife had a really positive relationship and were clearly in love with one another. He was attracted to her because in his opinion, she was a beautiful, smart, kind, and loyal woman who came from a close-knit family headed by a married father and mother who were a model for what he envisioned for his own family. However, in the early years of their marriage, financial struggles distracted them and limited their ability to focus on their relationship. Although there was never a threat of divorce or separation, the relationship was not growing the way that either Jeff or his new wife had expected. Things began to change when Jeff's business started to get off the ground. As a result, the more money they made, the more freedom they had to concentrate on growing together as a couple. Jeff explains, "about the beginning of year three, we really started to see things to make this climb. Which took off financial stress, you know, all those different things. Which allowed us to be able to turn back toward each other and not work."

Similarly, Reggie who was a 37-year-old, divorced, but dating barber and father of two at the time of his initial interview, also married the woman that he was dating at the outset of the study. However, for Reggie, this was a second marriage. In response to being asked how he met his current wife, Reggie described the process of making significant changes in his life in a number of areas. Consistent with this philosophy, Reggie mentions being attracted to his now wife because she was different than what he was accustomed to generally and different from his ex-wife specifically. Also, like Jeff, Reggie reported being appreciative of the support that his wife provided to him in his decision to go back to school so that he could run his salon more effectively.

I'd been through a divorce, so I made some changes, went to a new church. Actually, the church I used to go to 2 years ago with my ex-wife, and then she had some problems there, so I left. I really liked the church, so I went back to the church. I don't know, she [current wife] was just different. She was from West Virginia. She was just different, you know? From what I'm used to being with as far as me and her qualities. Her own mindset, and her own whole demeanor . . . just something that's different, you know? I was divorced, I had started working on my health. I had lost like 70 pounds, and I was just trying to make an overall change. That seemed like it just fell in to place. I mean she was just different. I guess what it was, I would always be with different chicks and they would want you to do this and do that. I wasn't used to being around somebody who was willing to do for me just like I do for them. And then luck hit, that was the other thing that played a part was a lot of these females, they want you to take care or do for their kids, but they wasn't there for yours. The support, having my back. A lot of times, her and her desires have helped me reach my goals and be the man I'm trying to be. . . . You know, I'm a barber and a hairstylist, so I own a salon next door. I decided I want to go to hair school because I got tired of depending on other people to run my salon. I decided I wanted to go to hair school to get my license to run the salon off my license. You talk about fresh into marriage, jumping off into school full time. She held me down for two years.

Jake's relationship trajectory also included a transition to marriage over the study period. However, unlike Jeff and Reggie, he was not romantically involved with his now wife during his initial interview. At that time, he was dating a different woman who he described as someone he could see himself settling down with. Despite this favorable characterization and stated interest in marriage, Jake broke up with his girlfriend before eventually proposing to his current wife, a woman he knew from grade school who he reconnected with after a serendipitous encounter online. Below, Jake explains this process and what attracted him to his current wife.

> When you talked to me last time, I was a young adult, in my social prime . . . I had been doing a lot of things, been around a lot of people, very social individual. Liked to be out, hanging out, doing stuff like that. I'm just not that person anymore. I've grown up, and realized I only wanted to be with one person, and things just started to make sense. Like I said, when you meet an amazing person, you don't really think twice about it. It wasn't anything that shaped my experiences. It was running into the right person and wanting to be a better person so that they would be around for a long time. . . . She has a great personality. She's extremely helpful. She's probably the best teammate I've ever had in my life. She's always teaching me things to help me be a better person, make myself better, and more dynamic. She helps me make responsible decisions, and she's always there when I need her. Yeah, she all the way had her stuff together. While I thought I was on top of my game, she really showed me what handling business looked like. For me, that was a big thing because I wasn't necessarily ready to adjust when I met her, but I knew that I wanted to spend the rest of my life with her. I was willing to make whatever changes were necessary to do that.

Next were Ronald and Wayne. Perhaps of all the men experiencing any relationship transitions, theirs were the most unlikely given their attitudes at the start of the study. For both Ronald and Wayne, not only were they not dating anyone at the start of the study, but they both expressed no interest in either marriage, an exclusive dating relationship, or any romantic relationship. Recall from chapter 4, Wayne shared that after his break up with his ex-girlfriend combined with the divorces in his family of origin, in his initial interview, his take on marriage was "why waste the time for real? . . . I'm thinkin' why in the world would I put myself in that position to be married and ultimately end up not being together in the long run." Similarly, Ronald, who was a 27-year-old college student at the time of his initial interview, had a perspective that could be best characterized as skeptical and reluctant on the topics of dating and marriage. However, in exploring their relationship trajectories, their narratives revealed significant changes of heart. Given the significant shift in their thinking around marriage, there was interest in learning more about the circumstances that contributed to their respective changes of heart. In the following final follow up interview excerpts, Ronald and Wayne open up about their relationship transitions. For Ronald, the fact that his wife did not display traits and qualities that he had strong aversions to made him open to dating her.

> She was independent, she pretty much . . . she wasn't one of those people that was ghetto. She had her own place, she was always at church. She was, like you said, she's mild mannered. She wasn't one of those loud people and all that. Well, she's pretty caring, she gets off work before I do so usually dinner is on the table. We both share the same things, we both like to travel . . . I mean, she does what a typical wife, what society says a wife is supposed to be. Cleans the house and everything, all that. I mean I help out, but you know I'm in school full time and I work full time. I have school three days a week, after work so with her taking up the slack, it's pretty cool.

In Wayne's case, after a rough break up with a woman with whom he had cohabited only to find out she had been unfaithful, he reconnected with a former co-worker with whom he always had a good relationship. Although the relationship was originally platonic, as he explains, it was the foundation of trust and familiarity along with the revelation that they had common core values that made dating and ultimately marriage a viable possibility.

> It [relationship with previous girlfriend] hadn't worked out, so I was really hesitant about doing it this time. Well it was I got into a relationship with someone and it progressed over a period of years actually. We had a child, it seemed I guess it was right to go ahead and get married as well. It wasn't like we hadn't talked about being married or something like that. It was more of a situation of is this the time to get married? We had been talking about it for so long, it was kind of go ahead and do it. It was really just that, I guess it was just that it was kind of familiar. I knew the kind of person that she was before, what happened is a situation where she continued to be there for me. She's honest, she's loyal, she's always trying to help you out whenever I needed help. I always try to help her out too. There was always a safety there. It made sense for me because there's just a lot of girls that I thought were for me [but they weren't], somebody that I could actually see myself being with. We were kind of similar in ways.

Not all of the men who experienced relationship transitions entered into a new dating relationship or elevated their dating relationship to marriage. Three of the men went from being involved in a romantic relationship to being single. In the case of Paul, who described himself as a "hopeless romantic," he was in a serious committed relationship to a woman who he later got engaged to. However, they broke up before they got married. He subsequently met a new partner, got engaged to her, but they also broke up before ever marrying. On the other hand, Adam and Rex were in relationships at the start of the study that eventually dissolved. When this happened, for varying reasons, they both decided to remain single. As Adam explains the breakup with the woman he was dating at the start of the study, as well as another woman that he dated for a few months, he describes how he then turned his attention to focusing on his career. In doing so, he did not leave much time to pursue or maintain a romantic relationship.

> She wanted to get married, and I didn't. That's the bottom line on that. That young lady, she pressured me, too, to the point where she got married. Both of the girls ended up getting married. The first one was just the one I talked to you about. She ended up marrying her ex-husband but wasn't happy. She ended up getting married. Then she got divorced in less than a year because she wasn't happy. I'm a career man right now, and in my business it's really tough for women to understand. I'm in the film industry and stuff, and I've been in that industry for about 29 years. I focus on my work, but it takes a lot of time. Women require much time. The number one thing, they require is time, really. They might say, "Nah, it's okay. I understand." That only lasted for a little while. They need that time, and I get busy. Man, that's always been the issue with me probably especially in the last three years. I started my new business three years ago, a film production company. I don't even entertain women that much. I don't egg them on or nothing like that because I don't want to be in a relationship with them because right now, I'm focused on my career. I'm on lock down with my work. One day she said, "Am I your girl?" You know how they do it. "Am I your girl?" I was like, "What do you mean *my* girl? Like I'm your girl? You my man?" She was like, "Yeah." I was like . . . I said, "I can't be nobody's man right now." That's what I told her straight up. Can't really be nobody's man right now. I'll be there for you if you need something. I'll pray for you. Do all that good stuff. As far as being the man thing, I said . . . at that point, it was a wrap.

Here, Adam makes it clear that getting romantically involved is not in his plans. After his breakup, Rex was also of the mind that he did not want to pursue a new romantic relationship, albeit for different reasons. While Adam was making a conscious decision to prioritize his career, Rex was taking time to be alone so that he could do some reflective work about how and why his former girlfriend cheated on him on.

> Right now, I'm not dating anybody, and with that relationship, things have fallen apart, and we were together for a little bit over 3 years. Things went really well, and we were really clicking, but I guess I'll say you let me know if you need me to expound upon anywhere there, but kind of long story short about it is she ended up cheating on me. Yeah, she ended up cheating on me there, and that was going on there for a couple months towards the end of our relationship. I found out after-the-fact, and so she actually had cheated on me with another girl. It was actually a sorority sister of hers. Yeah, and so that happened. . . . It didn't seem like the relationship was a priority, or it didn't seem like we were getting anywhere no matter how many conversations we had about ending the problem we were trying to fix, my half or her half, and then after a while it's just like, "No, you're not happy in this. I'm not happy in this. Let's cut it off." She didn't feel like I was always there, and I didn't feel like she was always there and present, and later I found out why. . . . Some girls need additional attention, more than the average, and so I feel like if she did mean that much to me, I could have provided more to really keep her in my life. It was important to me for me to finish grad school . . . I had a lot of transitions going on in my life, and I kind of just . . . I guess I took her for granted, you could say, as if like, oh yeah, she's going to be there, so I didn't put that much time into it. In hindsight, I feel like that should be the number one thing I was putting the time and energy towards, maybe not fraternity friends and all this other stuff.

As Rex shared his story, he discussed how his relationship was steadily deteriorating before he found out about the infidelity. Interestingly, he also recalled how his ex-girlfriend seemed distracted and not fully "present." While doing so, he acknowledges that he could have been more attentive and present for her so that she would not feel taken for granted. However, at the time, he chose to prioritize his studies and fraternity. Ultimately, he was left wondering if those were the correct choices.

The last of the relationship transitions that were experienced involved men who were either married at the start of the study or got married soon after the study started, only to experience a separation before the end of the study. This was the case for three of the men and of these men, two of them got back together with their wives while the third was still separated at the end of the study. First there was Nick who ended up separating from his wife for 18 months after being married for only 2 years. In his initial interview, Nick talked about some of the challenges facing his marriage and how many of them stemmed from the baggage that both he and wife brought from previous relationships. Chief among these challenges was the fact that their relationship trauma made it difficult for them to establish trust. This was exacerbated by the fact that both Nick and his wife had lived alone as adults for so long that they each had children with other partners and had established their own households prior to meeting, dating, and ultimately marrying. The combination of the trust issues and the years of independence made the negotiation that was necessary for them to come together as a unit in a single household very difficult. In the quote below, Nick recalls the circumstances leading up to the separation.

> We've been married for a few years, we also had separated in that time, and so now we are starting to . . . almost to get to know each other again. That would be a right thing, but more so, we're starting to learn to appreciate each other. . . . Yeah, I think that the issues that led up to the separation, because on my end I didn't trust her when it came to us making decisions. I thought she was making decisions that she thought was in her best interest and not in the best interest of the whole. She was still operating in terms of "I," and you asked me this earlier, she was operating like she was before we got married, because she was a single mom and because she bought her house as a single woman, she was so used to doing everything on her own. . . . Yeah. Then on my end, I would say, "Well I'm not going to do this, then. I'm not going to do this because you want me to," so I started being stubborn and not being a team player as well. It was just both of us then, you know, stupid. Both of us would get crazy.

After an extended separation of 18 months, Nick and his wife were able to work through their relationship issues by going back to "get to know each other again." In this process, rather than focusing on the courtship and emotions, they chose to spend their time working on being more selfless, emphasizing collective decision making, and building trust.

Like Nick, Keith and his wife also experienced a separation during the study period. In their case, the separation lasted 6 months although the challenges leading up to the separation began much earlier. In discussing the circumstances surrounding the separation, Keith pointed to financial stressors, as well as the transition to parenthood and his own behavior as reasons for the separation.

> Yeah we did. We separated. My son was born in August. August 19th. We split right around December. She didn't come back to the house 'til right around May or June. She actually left the house for that long. Technically in my mind we was split a few months before then because we really weren't talking, we were sleeping in separate rooms and things like that when she got up and left the crib. Right around that time and she was off from the house for like 6 months. That's when the recession had hit. My wife had lost her job. We had got laid off twice in a year. We was having a baby. I was driving a school bus. I wasn't making enough money. I was in school. I wasn't home a lot. I really wasn't catering to her needs and her being pregnant and things like that. Then after we had the

child, I was trying to balance being a new father, still be in school, still working and I thought I was doing what I needed to and in actuality I wasn't from
my standpoint. Like when I come home from a hard days work and my wife
wanted to talk to me just simply sitting down and talk or ask her how her day
went or ask her how . . . or help her out with the newborn child or come home
at a decent hour. If I got off work at 5:30 instead of coming home at 6, I would
come home at 10. She'd be like, "where was you at?" I was just kicking it. I felt
that I've been at work all day I needed to unwind, cool, but at the same time she
has been with a newborn all day.

In his final follow up interview, Keith looked back at his separation and
admitted that at the time, he was not doing nearly enough to support his
wife after the birth of their child. In discussing his lack of support, he not
only mentioned financial support, but also emotional support. In his initial
interview, he talked about how early in his marriage, his wife's independence
threatened his sense of masculinity and caused him to feel like less of a man
because he was accustomed to being a person that his family of origin could
rely on. Therefore, being laid off represented another blow to his ego, leading
him to spend more time away from home so as to not confront his problems.
As Keith readily acknowledged, he recognized that there were problems with
the relationship, but addressing them only became urgent when his wife left
and went to live with her mother. It was at that time that the potential loss
of relationships with his wife and child got his attention, so much so that he
admits "sweating" his wife by stopping by her mother's home to see her and
their child almost every day. Eventually, his mother-in-law convinced his
wife to return home to work on her relationship, an act that Keith was grateful
for, considering that he and his mother-in-law had not always seen eye-to-eye
in the past.

Finally, we have Sean who had been married for nine years but was separated at the end of the study. As he shared his narrative, he admitted feeling
confused by the entire situation. To be specific, Sean was confused because
his opinion was that his wife was no longer affectionate with him. He also
believed that she no longer put forth the level of effort into the marriage that
she once did, yet she was the one who initiated the separation.

The thing is that if one person wants to try to work things out and the other
person may want to work things out but not really try to put forth the effort then
that's what separates a marriage. I'm just saying that my wife was in a place she
wanted to separate. Me being the type of person, the man that I am, it's like, well
that's fine. Here's the thing is like when people don't recognize the fault within
themselves, you know what I'm saying? They look at somebody to blame. . . .
It's like the effort that I put forward in the marriage I don't feel that it's recip-
rocated. You know what I'm saying? It's one of those things where you know

how when you see certain couples and you look at them you can tell that they mesh well. That they're in love with each other. That they have a certain type of relationship that's not easily broken basically. . . . Those are the things where I don't feel like she, how I want to say it? When we out and about, sometimes if we at somebody's house, I may rub her feet. I rub her back, be affectionate. That's one thing I know she's not really affectionate at all in a sense not towards me. She's affectionate towards the boys, towards our kids. She's affectionate even to other people like at our church. She don't give that type of affection to me per se. Maybe she feels like we've been together long enough where she's comfortable. She don't feel like she has to show that type of affection towards me. You know what I'm saying. Me, she won't do that. You know what I'm saying. I have to ask her [as opposed to her initiating affection on her own]. You know what I'm saying? Maybe more than once.

Nick, Keith, and Sean all experienced a separation during the study. However, Nick and Keith were able to work with their wives to resolve their respective issues and resume their marriages. This was not the case for Sean whose issues seemed more dire from the perspective that in owning their role in the problems, Nick and Keith could contribute to the solution. However, for Sean, according to him, his wife was exclusively to blame for their marital problems. The fact that she was also the person who wanted the separation meant that he was essentially rendered powerless to work toward resolution.

## RELATIONSHIP STABILITY

The remaining 17 (53%) men reported no changes in their partners or relationship status over the study period. This romantic stability was represented by men who were single across the entire study period, as well as those who were either involved in a dating relationship or marriage to the same partner for the duration of the study. A total of three of the men were divorced or single at the start of the study and remained that way. Among these men was Alex, an 18-year-old college student at time of the initial interview who remained single throughout the duration of study. According to Alex, although he was not actively pursuing one, he was not against entering into a romantic relationship. In response to being asked his opinion about why he remained single over the course of the study, Alex stated, "I stay to myself a lot." As he continued, he mentioned that he had a few female friends and some where there was some mutual interest. However, he stated that he has often been told that he was "too guarded and that I need to be more emotional and say how I feel more." This became problematic because being or feeling pushed to talk about his feelings was a turn off for Alex who stated, "I don't know, I've just always been like that. I don't like talking about emotions."

Tyrone and Thomas were also single across the entire study period. However, unlike Alex, they were single as a result of divorcing prior to the start of the study. At 72, Tyrone, a retired attorney with two adult children, was the oldest participant in the study. In sharing his story, he talked about having been divorced in his 40s, well before the start of the study. In reflecting on his divorce, he shared, "I came of age at a time when people got married young. In our case, probably before we really knew each other. Hell, in all honesty, it was before we knew our own selves." As he went on, he talked about he and his ex-wife growing apart, but making a decision to stay together until their children finished college. Tyrone talked about how after their kids graduated and left the house, the "glue" was gone. Therefore, he and his ex-wife decided to divorce because in their estimation, their children had what they needed to support themselves and they would no longer have to feel guilty about negatively impacting their educational pursuits by upsetting them with the fallout from a divorce. In discussing why he never remarried, Tyrone concluded that although he and his ex-wife had an amicable divorce and that they were both still active in their children's and grandchildren's lives including co-attending family functions, the concept of marriage never really truly resonated with him. To be specific, he shared, "Ahh . . . I don't know, maybe I was ahead of my time. But I never really believed that we would always be together. Like always? So, by the time I divorced, I was established and there wasn't pressure to get married again, so I didn't." For Tyrone, his divorce appeared to be more liberating than injurious. In this way, although Tyrone lamented what he called "wilting under the societal expectation to marry," he never held any animus toward his ex-wife. He just felt that marriage was not for him. However for Thomas, his divorce appeared to be a little more damaging from the standpoint that the circumstances surrounding his divorce made him reluctant to give serious consideration to new relationships because of the ways in which he felt his ex-wife questioned and devalued his leadership role in their relationship. In providing an update on his love life as a part of his final follow up interview, Thomas discussed the impact of his divorce and opened up about his lack of interest in pursuing any new relationships.

> I'm still single. I'm not romantically involved in any relationship. I guess I do have a female friend, but we're just friends. We're not romantically involved. I was married for 14 1/2 years, almost 15 years. There was some expectations of what she wanted at that particular time that were not met. I think that sort of added to the, I guess, her sense of disappointment and frustration. I think it's connected to that. I don't think it's necessarily growing apart. I think she simply, at that point in her life, at that point in the relationship, had some expectations that she felt should have been met. When they weren't, based on what her mind set was, and I guess her value system at that time, it was something that was

obviously, in a sense, that was intolerable, that she couldn't tolerate or permit. As a result of that, there was this disdain. So, I think at this point I'm leaning towards, perhaps, not ever getting married again.

Although a small minority of the men whose relationship status remained stable across the entire study period were single, the majority (14 of 17) of the men whose relationship status remained stable were either married or re-married at the start of the study and remained that way with the same partner through the conclusion of the study. With these men, there was interest in having them share their perspectives on the factors contributing to the stabil-ity of their marriages. In doing so, the men pointed to the core values that they shared with their partners, their efforts to get connected with men who were also married, and the ways in which having the experience of overcoming personal or collective adversity served to bring them closer to one another.

## Shared Values

The most frequently identified stabilizing factor that the men discussed was shared or common values. To be specific, shared values served to buttress the men's relationships in two ways. First, having a set of common values provided the men and their partners with a foundation from which to grow and nurture their relationship. Second, having the common core values also served to give the couples a set of guiding principles to give them direction if and when their relationships were tested. Most often, shared values came via the couples' religion. Joe and Terrell's interviews feature quotes illustrating these points. According to Joe:

> The Bible says you just have to love one another. Family comes first. I got two children, three grandchildren so they're the joy of my life right now. My wife and I, we don't have any secrets from each other. No, we don't keep any secrets. Know and respect each other, that's the main thing. It's not always about you, it's about others so you put others first and you'll get what's coming to you. She loves me and she's a Christian lady. We both think alike. Just took our vows serious I guess you could say. Right now, I've been down for about a year and a half. I have had five surgeries and every time I go to the hospital, she stays at the hospital every night. They moved me to a rehab place, she stayed over every night. We just done grew together.

To drive home the salient role that religion plays in their lives, Joe shares that he and his wife do not keep any secrets. He even went so far as to say that he did not care if she was listening in on the interview because she already knows all of his answers. Moreover, he goes on to argue that for both he and his wife, based on their Christian values, they both put family first. As a result of the selflessness, Joe believes that one will always "get what's coming to you." Finally, Joe credits his wife with never leaving his side as he struggled with myriad health concerns and surgical procedures. Following in that vein, Terrell also pointed to religion as a stabilizing factor in his relationship. Also, like many of the other men whose marriages remained intact over the course of the study period, Terrell also talked about his wife as a positive influence who kept him accountable being a better husband, father, and person.

> We both go to church every Sunday. We have our own way of getting together. Our relationship is not the same as everybody else. She had the same qualities that I have. She comes from a two parent home, she wanted better things in life, not just what was provided. She got her education, and she enforced me to go back to school and get my education in barbering. I was just a regular old factory worker. She told me, "The only way that me and you are going to be together is you got to get a solid foundation." I'll tell anybody, when I got my woman, she turned me into a whole other direction. If I hadn't ran into my wife, I'd probably still be living with my mother and father. Communication, the Lord, and the people that you surround yourself around, because you're going to need a support system on everything that you do.

According to the men whose relationships remained stable across the entire study period, in addition to the ways in which having a set of commonly shared core values served to help the men build a foundation for their relationships, connecting with a group of men who were in similar life stages or situations was also identified as an important stabilizing factor. In pointing this out, the men sought to emphasize the importance of minimizing temptation and exposure to behavior that might be perceived as questionable or unbecoming of a man in a committed relationship. For example, William mentioned:

> In order to protect, if you're married, you have to protect your marriage. You tend to hang around guys who are married, because guys who are married tend to have the same, best interest you have in terms of, you don't talk about other women. Your focus is how to build a family, personal property, your jobs, what's the best thing for your kids. We have those kinds of conversations. With a single person, you tend to, you talk about women. Going out, and the objective is to deal with women, unless you're in a stable relationship with somebody. Even if you're not, you still have those liberties. Married men, even if they're inclined to play like that, they really won't discuss it with other married guys, as much. That's something that you just don't talk about too much.

Beyond simply steering clear of potentially negative situations, connecting with and spending more time with other romantically involved and married men was also invoked as a strategy to receive mentoring and modeling from men who could offer valuable advice based on the similarities in their circumstances and life experiences. Amir's quote is representative of this sentiment that was expressed by several men.

> Consequently, I was able to re-network my life. The guys that were in my phone are no longer in there. I got new guys in my phone. The guys that were in my life are no longer in my life. I have new guys in my life. Guys that are married, that have been married, guys that are in the community. I had the opportunity not just to change my life but to change my peer group. That's made all the difference. What I would say, always being a husband is always thinking of your family. It's like lions. When they don't have a family, they run around with other males until they find a female. Until they start their own family. I see a lot of guys still doing that. They adults but they still running around with the pack instead of starting their own family.

Here, Amir shares his perspective on how he intentionally sought out married men in his community to connect with. For him, these men were examples of the types of family-centric changes that he wanted to make in his attitudes and behavior. In this way, he has been encouraged by the men around him to stop "running around with the pack" in favor of settling down and starting his own family.

The final stabilizing factor that emerged from the men's narratives was the support that they received from their girlfriends or wives during personally challenging times. These bouts with adversity included health concerns, dealing with the death of loved ones, financial stress, and custody battles with ex-wives and former partners. When these obstacles emerged, the men were clear about how much they appreciated their wives standing by their sides to help them manage and cope. In some cases, wives provided emotional support that signaled that they were in their men's corner or had his back. In chapter 4, Jeff talked about feeling needy and wanting constant reassurance from his wife while his business was struggling. He also talked about how much this support meant to him and how it served to solidify their bond. Similarly, Peter talked about receiving the same type of support and encouragement from his wife after he lost his job in the financial services industry and he decided to go back to school to become a teacher.

> She's like, baby don't worry about it. I know you're going to get another job and make money. We'll cut back where we can. I know you're not going to sit on your ass. Our relationship in this situation . . . this setback has strengthened our relationship, I feel, in a lot of ways. That's part of the reason I married my wife, because she's been there before. It's probably not as financially rewarding, but I think I'll be more happy and spend more time with my family and my kids. She's supportive of that.

Not only did the men's wives provide emotional support, but they also took active roles in helping their husbands through trying times. Consider Josh's quote. In his initial interview, he spoke about the fact that he had no intention to pursue a relationship with the woman that became his wife when they met. He even shared that for years into their relationship, he was unfaithful. In his follow up interviews, he expressed concern that his wife did not trust him and that she harbored anger and resentment for years even after his infidelity stopped, leading him to question whether his wife actually loved him or not. However, when he was diagnosed with cancer, his wife played a major role in helping him work though the mental and physical challenges.

> I was diagnosed with Leukemia. It took me all the way down. Just for my wife to be, like I said, to be a listener. You're laying in bed, that's the first night we had a conversation, and you sleep with somebody every night. And I remind her of that from time to time. We need to talk like we did that night. When I got sick, she stepped up and she did what she had to do. And I think that was part of the sickness too, to show my value. And she seen, cause it's like, when I was in the hospital, I know she love the shit out of them boys [the couple's sons], but that's when I knew she loved me 'cause she never left my bedside.

In recalling the ways that his wife was there for him during his diagnosis and subsequent treatment, Josh expressed a lot of guilt for his past transgressions. He even admitting wondering if his diagnosis was a punishment for all of the things he had done in his past. Nevertheless, when reflecting on the factors that facilitated the stability of his marriage, he cited his wife and her selflessness in caring for him and their children.

## CONCLUSION

The purpose of this chapter was to chronicle the men's relationship trajectories over time. Data analysis revealed that close to half of the study participants experienced at least one relationship transition in the 4-year study period. These transitions included three men going from not being involved in a romantic relationship to having a serious girlfriend, five men went from being divorced or single to being married, four men who went from being involved in a romantic relationship to breaking up and remaining single, and three men who were married but experienced a separation during the study period. Although these transitions were more likely for men who were younger, they occurred for men across the age and socioeconomic spectrums. As such, there were some other, more well-defined patterns that emerged to explain the reasons for the transitions. For the men whose transition represented the establishment of a new romantic relationship or formalizing an existing relationship by marrying, there were a few contributing factors. In several cases, the men were single after a breakup or divorce when they connected with women who were very different in terms of personality, disposition, and temperament from the men's former partners. So strong was the men's interest in moving away from women like their former partners that they spoke specifically about the fact they were in some ways attracted to their new partner because they were a departure from their exes. In addition to finding women who were different from their former partners, serendipitous encounters with women from the men's past also emerged as an important factor in their willingness to pursue a new relationship or entertain the idea of marriage. In each of these cases, the women were not former lovers, but instead were described as friends or acquaintances. The reconnections happened as a result of social media and people moving back to town after having left in early adulthood. Given the strong negative reactions that many of the men had to their former partners, it stands to reason that several of them would find solace in reconnecting with women with whom they were familiar and comfortable.

As for the men whose transition featured a breakup or separation, shifting priorities and challenges with reciprocity and empathy were identified as the dissolved relationships' root causes. According to these men, as things in the relationship changed over time and they, as well as with their partners, eventually found themselves placing emphasis on different areas. For some of the men, there was not agreement about whether to take the relationship to the next level. For other men, competing priorities led to the couple being distracted, not focused on one another, and ultimately infidelity became an issue. Men who were married and experienced a separation during the study period were also included in the discussions of relationship transitions. In each of these relationships, mistrust and a lack of empathy or reciprocity were implicated as the primary contributing factors. For two of these men, it was other transitions including becoming new parents or moving in together after having lived independently for years that exposed one or both partners' initial inability to empathize with what the other was experiencing that led to mistrust and contempt. In the third example, a lack of reciprocity and empathy was presented as a challenge. However, according to Sean, he bore no responsibility for his marital problems. In sharing his story, it was his wife who had become complacent, would no longer show him affection, and wanted the separation.

On the other hand, just a little over half of the men's relationship statuses remained stable over the entire study period. In a few cases, the relationship stability was an absence of any relationship immediately before, during, and at the end of the study. For these men, being averse to talking about emotions, in the case of Alex, Tyrone's philosophical differences with the societal emphasis placed on marriage, and the fallout from what seemed to be an impactful divorce for Thomas were the reasons cited for there being no interest in pursuing a romantic relationship. However, for most of the men, relationship stability was represented by the presence of an intact marriage that pre-dated the start of the study and did not experience any disruption or separation. For these men, having shared core values, having a peer network that included other married men, and having experienced some adversity that tested, but did not break the relationship proved to be important stabilizing factors. In many ways, as the men described them, shared values, spending time with other married men, and collectively triumphing over adversity all served to create a solid foundation from which the relationship could grow. With regard to shared values, religion was often invoked as creating a blueprint or script that guided the men and their wives' relationship thinking and behavior. This was best explained by Chad, a man who was remarried to the woman who he credited with helping him "turn his life around" because she introduced him to Christ. In discussing how shared values provided a base for his relationship, Chad made his marriage analogous to an isosceles triangle with God at the point and he and his wife on either side. In doing so, he stated that as long as both he and his wife were working to get closer to God, they would also naturally be coming closer together. Beyond shared values, the men whose marriages stayed stable across the study talked about the ways in which being around other married men served as a protective factor. This occurred because it provided the men with a source of social support that was uniquely positioned to understand what they were experiencing and could also provide relevant and appropriate advice. Moreover, other married men could be viewed as role models for how one could or should comport themselves in the context of their relationships. Further, to the extent that there was an expectation that married men refrain from pursuing and engaging women, spending time with other married men was posited as a way to insulate oneself from temptation or potentially precarious situations. Finally, experiencing and overcoming adversity was mentioned as a stabilizing factor that bolstered the foundation of the men's marriages. In these situations, the men talked about how having their marriages withstand the tests of financial difficulties, health concerns, and personal tragedy helped them to understand the strength and depth of their relationships with their wives. This was the case because most often, the men identified their wives as the person exhibiting the most strength in the face of adversity. Whether providing reassurance to Peter during his period of unemployment, Terrell's wife remaining strong after multiple miscarriages, or Josh's wife providing care in response to his Leukemia diagnosis, it was these tests that created the circumstances that compelled the couples to focus on one another that strengthened their bond and solidified for the men that their wife was in it for the proverbial long haul. In sum, there was no doubt that whether positive or negative, the experiences surrounding the men came to shape their relationship trajectories over time. However, what remained unclear was whether or not their relationship status came to define the participants as men. Therefore, chapter 6 focuses on an examination of the men discussing the extent to which being in a romantic relationship or marriage shaped their concept of masculinity.

## Chapter Six

# Love and Manhood

In the recently published, *Out of Knowledge of Self: Black Masculinity, Psychopathology, and Treatment,* Kniffley, Brown, and Davis (2018) argue that black men are the least understood of all sex-race groups in America's past and present. Therefore, in addition to discussing the roles of sex, previous trauma, and relationship transitions in shaping their relationship experiences and perspectives, there was also interest in better understanding the men's concepts of masculinity. To solicit their perspectives in this area, the men were queried about whether or not being in a romantic relationship or marriage was central to their sense of manhood. In other words, to what extent did the men in the study feel that being in a romantic relationship or marriage was important in shaping their masculine identities. This is an important question because like many other areas, there has been research featuring analyses of black masculinity, but as with many of these other areas, seldom has this research given voice to black men and provided them an opportunity to tell their own stories. It is also true that the extant representations of blackness that are currently available do not account for the full range of intersectional impacts of class, gender, sexuality, and age that are critical identity developing factors (Whiteneir 2019). Instead, most of the research has been based on theoretical reviews that fail to take both traditional and non-traditional masculine ideologies into consideration (Pierre, Mahalik, and Woodland 2001). An exploration of this research does reveal that the literature is focused largely on how college enrollment and socioeconomic status are known to shape black men's masculine identities, as well as research on the ways in which those masculine identities manifest themselves in black men's romantic relationships.

## FACTORS SHAPING BLACK MASCULINITY

Much of the research on factors shaping black men's masculine identities has been concentrated on black male college students (Brooms, Clark, and Smith 2018) or young adult black men residing in economically disadvantaged urban areas (Anderson 1990). With regard to the studies featuring college students, Harris, Palmer, and Struve (2011) explored the factors shaping and meanings ascribed to masculinity among a group of students enrolled at a private research university. Their findings revealed that concepts such as toughness, aggressiveness, material wealth, responsibility, and restrictive emotionality defined their sense of masculinity. Moreover, the men discussed that their masculinity was expressed behaviorally through striving to take advantage of leadership and academic opportunities. Unfortunately, the authors concluded that the men's masculinity was also expressed through homophobia, fear of femininity, and the constrained relationships with women that they experienced. Goodwill et al. (2019) interviewed black men from a midwestern university about their perceptions of masculinity. In response to questions about their identity, the men referred to well-known media figures, athletes, and entertainers who were central to their conceptualizations of masculinity. This finding led the authors to conclude that popular cultural figures play complex roles in black men's ideas about manhood. Mincey et al. (2015) surveyed black men at both a Historically Black College and University (HBCU) and a Predominantly White Institution (PWI) and found that both subsets of men agreed that to be a man means that one "takes care of business, handles responsibility, and provides for his family" (p.325).

In keeping consistent with the theme of taking care of business and providing for one's family, the existing literature also includes several studies that explore the ways in which social and economic disadvantage shape black men's masculine identities. As with most of these studies, Malton (2010) and hooks (2004) explain that in both historical and contemporary contexts, black men's inability to access the mainstream labor market has relegated them to a marginalized status in their communities and families. As they seek to confront their exclusion from the capitalist economic system that rewards patriarchy and dominance, many low income black men prioritize money and the acquisition of it regardless of how it is obtained, leading some to adopt a street masculinity. An example of this was Roy and Dyson's (2010) qualitative study of 75 low income black fathers in which they found that the participants held normative and traditional expectations for successful manhood vis-à-vis men from other races and income levels. However, their low income status made living up to these expectations difficult because they resided in communities that offered few opportunities to gain a sense of control or mastery over their lives and life chances. In response, rather than acting in a way that manifested their masculine identity, the men spent their time fighting for daily survival and resisting the stigma and stereotypes associated with coming from low income, urban areas. Similarly, Hammond (2012) explored the relationship between racial discrimination and depressive symptoms among black men and found that adherence to masculine norms prevented men from being emotionally expressive. In addition, their preoccupation with self-reliance hindered their ability to confide in those in their personal network, including intimate relationships. As a result, the relationships most at risk for being damaged by the black men's adoption of masculine norms and their associated emotional restrictions were their romantic relationships and marriages.

## Black Masculinity and Romantic Relationships

In his book, *From Brotherhood to Manhood*, Franklin (2004) argues that black men are largely invisible to the broader society. However, one of the ways for black men to gain visibility is through their association with women whose appearances they believe will find approval within their critical networks. This is even more so the case if the woman's physical appearance meets criteria for beauty promoted by white society. Therefore, the choice of a partner, one of the few things black men have some control over, is vital to their status and self-esteem. Franklin further argues that demonstrating the ability to get a girl is the first major test of manhood for teenage boys. In pursuit of this goal, black boys often find willing mentors in their fathers, older brothers, uncles, and friends. Franklin concludes that the dreadful downside of this mentoring is that it transforms the black woman into a conquest rather than a partner.

Equally problematic is the fact that black men who are socialized in traditional contexts oftentimes have male role models who regularly devalue women (Peters et al. 2010) leading them to adopt many of the patriarchal and oppressive ideologies that necessitate that there are dominant and submissive figures in relationships. This occurs as black women and men, like their white American counterparts, endorse "family myths" or the belief that each spouse should perform the tasks that they are better at while, because of their socialization into traditional gender specific roles, each are better at traditionally gendered tasks (Dixon 2014). However, the Eurocentric definition of being the head of the household does not incorporate the more egalitarian role that seems to be part of the process in black family functioning. Therefore, the roles of both black men and women can appear distorted. For example, black men are often seen as passive, unreliable, and irresponsible while black women are viewed as being too overbearing, controlling, and unfeminine in their roles within their relationships. Their prominent role of helping to sustain the family and the relationship by actively participating in economic provisions of the home is seen as counterproductive to their relationship with the black male, while undermining his masculinity (Lawrence-Webb, Little-field, and Okundaye 2014).

So pervasive are these warped narratives that they have infiltrated the consciousness of large numbers of both black men and women. As such, Jewell (2014) asserts, it should not come as a surprise that many black men and women are prone to portraying and perceiving each other negatively, contributing to intrapersonal and interpersonal conflict for black males and females that has implications for feelings of worth and identity development. As many black Americans accept negative definitions assigned to them, it creates a circumstance that fosters distrust and skepticism at the inception of the relationship. Subsequently, all actions or behaviors engaged in during the relationship are evaluated on the basis of previously held definitions and perceptions.

These negative definitions and perceptions can be particularly damaging for black men because as Franklin (2004) explains, it is more common for men to feel that their women hold them back or stand in their path. As a result, black men tend to believe they need to handle things on their own while women are more likely to think of working together. Since men are also more likely to prioritize protection of their dignity, black men tend to place significant importance on their woman's compliance with their thinking because having people listen to them is important to their sense of self, identity, and power. Therefore, given the racism that many black men face, the private world they create with their women represents an oasis of dignity and self-respect. As a consequence, black men can be upset when they perceive that their mates are tampering with the safe haven that they have created. For these reasons, Franklin (2004) concludes that control is so much a part of being a man that when others, especially women, have more of a say in what they do and how they should live than they do, their instinct is to push back in defiance.

In sum, a review of the existing literature reveals that much of the research on black masculinity is theoretical (Hopkins and Moore 2006), deficit framed, or based on the experiences of socially dislocated and economically disadvantaged black men (Roy and Dyson 2010; Seaton 2007). Thus, it disproportionately focuses on the challenges facing black men and the ways in which those challenges shape their masculine identities, as well as how those identities are reflected through their attitudes and behavior in romantic relationships. In response, *Black Love Matters* includes the narratives of a more diverse group of men as it explores the connection between black men's involvement in romantic relationships and marriage and their masculine ideologies and identities.

## Relationship Influenced Masculinity

Of the 32 participants completing final follow up interviews, 20 (62.5%) of them reported that being involved in a romantic relationship or marriage was important to their concept of masculinity and manhood. In these cases, the men cited the ways in which being in relationships satisfied their need for companionship and desire for intimacy, being in a committed relationship helped to make them more responsible as men and fathers, and being in a relationship provided them with a structure for defining manhood.

In explaining how being in a romantic relationship shaped their concept of masculinity, some of the men took a practical approach, offering that their relationships satisfied their need for companionship and desire for intimacy. As was discussed in chapter 3, intimacy was something that many of the men coveted. Therefore, for those who prioritized intimacy, it stood to reason that intimate connections associated with romantic relationships would also shape their ideas around manhood and masculinity. As plainly stated by Sean, "every many has a desire to have a woman, because they're beautiful. I mean, a man should want that." Offering a little more detail, Chris shared the following:

> For me, to have been a single man and to maintain the Christian values that I think are so critical, I don't know how I could have done it. I'm such a physical touch guy, I don't know how I could have lived alone, which to me is the option that you have if you're not married. Christian wise, I think I would have made a mess of the ministry. I'm being honest. That's who I am. I know some guys could probably handle it okay. I think my wife probably could have made it as a person who never married. I could not have. We would often joke with each other that if she died, she said, "I know, you'd mourn for me for about six months, then you'd have another wife." In some ways she knows me best. I don't think it would be six months, but I don't think I would sit here in mourning for the rest of my life. Even in my 60s, I hope I'm going to live another 20 years or so. I think I would have probably still wanted companionship. I just don't like to be alone.

Keith also weighed in revealing that being married to his wife has allowed him a space to be his, true, authentic self with regard to his emotional expressiveness. Recall that in chapter 4, Keith shared that his socialization, particularly the way he was raised by his mother, did not promote being emotionally demonstrative. And it was this lack of emotion that contributed to the disconnect between he and his wife, ultimately leading to them being separated. In sharing that story, Keith also mentioned that contrary to how he was raised, he did not like to withhold his feelings. Here, he mentions how being married has allowed him to be free in that regard.

> I'm learning to get in touch with my more emotional side and breaking down that barrier for me. I needed that. You'll never know, if you're not close to me in my circle, you'll never see the inside of me. I never allow people to do it. I laugh and joke with my peers at work but they'll never get to see that real me. . . . Being married to my wife, it's allowed me to bring that out and let me know it's okay to let people in. I think me being that way comes from society, how I was raised and things like that.

Another rationale provided by the men for reporting that being in a relationship was important to their concept of manhood and masculinity was that being in a romantic relationship made them better and more responsible as men. In these cases, the men cited the benefits that have been associated with marriage and credited their mates with helping them settle down and holding them accountable for behaving maturely. First, Jake discussed what he sees as the connection between being married and his interest in becoming a better person. Specifically, he points to his wife as the person who keeps him focused on this goals.

> I always tell her that I couldn't have really done or become who I am without her. I mean that with every fiber of my being. The person that she is has continually helped me to become the person that I needed to be. For me, meeting the right person, to stand with the right person is probably the most important decision I've made in my life.

Amir goes a step further than Jake below as he not only describes the way being married changed him, but also led him to create different expectations for those around him.

> The commitment that comes with it [marriage]. How y'all can make a better life for each other, building together, the teamwork that comes with it. The intimacy. The respect. To me, being a husband is the highest form of being a man. I have different expectations for people and for myself now that I'm a husband.

In his quote, Amir alludes to the fact that once he became a married man, he created different expectations for himself and for the people in his circle of influence. In doing so, he talked about how he had to move away from some former friends and replace them with new peers, people whose life experiences were similar to his current situation. In doing so, Amir was making an attempt to be more accountable for thinking and behaving in ways that were consistent with what he felt would facilitate success in a committed relationship.

Furthermore, the notion of accountability was also a defining feature of other men's narratives. Illustrative of this was Josh who made the transition from a life exploiting woman to one that was family-centered and included a wife and kids. Below, he credits his wife with keeping him motivated during a particularly dark time in his life in which he was dealing with a lot of grief and loss.

> I think she [black women] is what we [black men] need. That's the prescription. Because when I was laying around, my jewelry store closed, I lost my momma so I was sad, I was in this slight depression. Yeah, when I think back to me laying around, as a black man, being lazy, you know, I'm kinda thinking the jewelry store is closed. She say you need to get a job . . . and I credit her, I never even told her this, but [she helped] when I got a job for ChemCo. She called, and said they hiring at ChemCo. I'm a grown man, but I'm out riding around on a moped, I'm out playing. She told me to ride over there. I walked in and said I'm here about the job. The manager told me, you have to fill out the application, but when you do, you got the job. I was thinking, damn, I don't want no job! But I did it too, you know, like to satisfy her. Got the job at ChemCo, worked. Got two years out there like part time, end up getting another clean up job, and I end up being the supervisor on the job after about a year. Next thing you know, I had my own building, my own crew. But it was from that push of that black woman.

Like many of the other men, Josh speaks to the central role that his wife played in helping him grow, evolve, and push through a difficult time in his life. Of particular interest, he places emphasis on the fact that his wife is a black woman as he mentions that black women specifically are what he and other black men need because of their ability to motivate and inspire black men.

Closely related to believing that being in a romantic relationship positively contributed to their sense of responsibility, several of the men also discussed the ways in which their involvement in their romantic relationships facilitated their involvement with their children. In the words of Amir, his marriage to his wife created space for him to "feel like a whole man. Being a father, being a man, being a husband and being involved with your family and your community." Another example was Terrell who had recently become a first-time father shortly before his last interview. Here, he weighed in on the ways in which his romantic relationship carved out opportunities for his involvement with his newborn son. As he explains, it is his marriage to his son's mother that he anticipates will serve as the pathway to leading him into manhood.

> My son, I feel like if he sees that I'm not being what I'm supposed to be around here at the house, then it's going to be kind of hard for him to figure out his

individual qualities of what he's supposed to be. If I'm not showing him the right way, then it's going to totally be backwards when it comes down for him, he's going to be confused and asking more questions.

The final rationale offered by the men who felt that being in a marriage or romantic relationship had implications for their conceptualization of masculinity was that their relationships provided them with parameters for shaping manhood by reinforcing gender roles. In other words, for these men, the presence of a romantic relationship went beyond merely shaping their concept of manhood and masculinity, it necessarily defined it. The following confirmatory quote from Rex is illustrative of this sentiment.

> That can be complicated, but I'll say yes, but it's also . . . I'll also say before I really dig into that, is that I still feel like you can be a man and still have all the assets of masculinity without being in a relationship, so I don't feel like you necessarily have to be framed on being a relationship and how you are in that relationship, but I think when we talk about masculinity and being a masculine man in the context of a relationship on what that means, what that looks like, I do think the relationship has a pretty pivotal role, because it's the role that you play within that relationship as a man . . . but honestly in the context of a relationship, I do think it's important as a man to be able to provide. I don't think it's your responsibility to be a sole provider, but I think that it's important that you're able to provide for your relationship and for your family.

In sharing his perspective, Rex describes being in a relationship as having a "pretty pivotal role" in shaping his concept of masculinity. He then goes on to talk about how his gender role performance is very traditional in nature as he places emphasis on financial provision and associates it with being a man. Also traditional in his thinking is Terrell. So much so that in his attempt to describe the ways in which his relationship with his wife defines his sense of masculinity, he simultaneously perpetuates a myth about the superiority heteronormative and patriarchal family structure while also rejecting the legitimacy of same sex relationships being recognized as marriages.

> With the way things are these days, I feel like the structure of marriage is totally changing. They saying nowadays, two women can be married, and call it a marriage. I don't feel it that way. I think it takes a man and a woman to call it marriage. I don't care what nobody says. I feel like a man's supposed to be at the top of the tier to make the family work. Sometimes, my wife don't feel that, but that's the way it is. Sometimes, we'll make changes and let her be at the top tier on certain things, but when it's all said and done, what's good for me and my wife is not good for others. As long as you sit down and talk about it, it don't always have to look like the man is out front. Sometimes it can be the woman out front, but it's the man's actual structure. It's just the man that brings it out.

I feel like a man . . . me being the man around at the house, keeps the structure of my house going the same. I don't care what nobody says. If you're going to build a family, build a relationship, you got to have a good man in that family.

Similarly, Dan also defined himself by his relationship. However, in his case, he attempted to use his relationship as a shield to mask his struggle with his sexuality by continuing to participate in a heterosexual relationship so as to avoid the ridicule that he perceived would come his way if those around him found out he was gay.

Yeah, right or wrong, healthy or unhealthy, the way I was raised was the way— not even just raised, like people in my family sitting down and talking to me, this is what makes you a man. That's not what we got. What I got was, men do this. Men are doers. You work, you pay bills, you have sex. . . . So what they tell you is to be a man is to do all those things, and anything that is the antith- esis of that is not manhood, so you can't be gay and still call yourself as much of a man as a straight guy. There's a spectrum of masculinity. Your goal is to be 100%. Certain things will knock you down from that 100% mark, and that's putting you closer to being . . . a woman, basically, which is what we don't want.

Whether due to satisfying their need for companionship and intimacy, feeling compelled to be more responsible as a man and father, or having their man- hood defined by it, being in a romantic relationship was reported as having significant implications for close to two-thirds of the study participants' con- cepts of masculinity. Although this represents the majority of the men in the study, a sizeable minority disagreed and felt that their sense of masculinity was not tied to their involvement in a romantic relationship or marriage. The following section details the men who held this position.

## Relationship Independent Masculinity

Although the majority of the men agreed that being in a romantic relationship or marriage was important in shaping their concept of masculinity, 12 of the 32 (37.5%) of the study participants disagreed. For these men, being a husband, boyfriend or intimate partner was not a defining feature of manhood. Instead, self-reliance and personal development were referenced as the factors impact- ing these men's perceptions of manhood. For other men, rejecting the notion that being in a romantic relationship shaped their concept of masculinity was grounded in the freedom and flexibility associated with being a single man. Perhaps most interesting, like the men who agreed that their romantic relation- ship helped to shape their identities as men, some of the men who said that relationships did not define their concepts of masculinity also cited behaving responsibly as men and fathers as defining features of their masculinity.

The salience of self-reliance was the most frequently referenced explanation given for how the men arrived at the conclusion that their identities as men were not shaped by the presence or absence of a romantic relationship. For example, in response to being asked if being in a romantic relationship shaped his masculine identity, Wayne stated, "Not necessarily. I was independent before I got married, so you know. Being married is good but you have to be happy with yourself first." The emphasis that Wayne placed on individual fulfillment was echoed by other men including Brandon, a 53-year-old married father and cook, who offered the following:

> No. Not in being a man. I think . . . I don't think they should be the same thing because I still got the opinion of if I wasn't married, I don't think that would make me any less of a man. I just feel like, maybe marriage isn't for everybody. Maybe people have issues with themselves or other people that would lend itself to be a unhealthy relationship with somebody else. I don't think that has anything to do with being a man . . . I think being able to handle your own crisis, or whatever without the assistance of anybody else, makes you more of a man or a woman than anything else. Not being dependent, I think makes you a man or woman.

Here, Brandon discusses how he would feel like a man regardless of whether he was in a romantic relationship or not. In other words, his concept of manhood is only dependent on things that he can control such as handling crises. And while he concedes that being in a relationship can add to this, he would not feel like less of a man in the absence of such a relationship. Next, Chad agrees that he need not be in a relationship to feel like a man. In fact, he is of the opinion that being in a negative relationship can have the effect of detracting from one's sense of value, worth, or identity. In offering the perspective that being in an unhealthy relationship can become a deterrent to engaging in subsequent relationships, Chad's opinion mirrors the experiences of several of the men highlighted in chapters 4 and 5 who admitted that their relationship trajectories were negatively altered as a result of having experienced earlier relationship trauma.

> I'm going to say . . . Is it important to the concept of being a man? I can be a man by myself. I feel like it helps me. I feel like marriage is a good thing. It's all about finding the right person for you. You can be with somebody that looks like, got the perfect body, this, that, and the other. She may not add to you, she may take from you. That's why sometimes, you see women and men, they're so drained from their relationship, they don't want another one. They feel like it's going to be the same. They feel like, I would put all my time, energy, and effort into this, and I'm going to leave with less than I came with.

In addition to identifying self-reliance and the pursuit of personal development rather than involvement in a romantic relationship as the factors impacting their concepts of masculinity, some of the men also talked about simply being content with being single. For these men, the sense of liberation associated with being single was enough to make them feel like men. Put plainly, Paul said, "I don't need a woman to validate me. It would be nice to have one woman that I could just be madly in love with, be married, and happy. But, at this point in time I can take the single life." This perspective was not surprising coming from Paul given the relationship difficulties that he experienced during the study period including multiple relationship transitions and engagements that never materialized. However, other participants who were not only in healthy romantic relationships, but even some who were married like Peter also attested to being satisfied with his sense of masculinity when he was single.

> I think, honestly, I was comfortable being single. When I met my wife, I wasn't looking for a relationship. Now I was 29, so I was getting to the point where the party lifestyle and hanging out with the fellas was getting old. I think maybe I was ready to get into a committed relationship. It's kind of like I met that person that was perfect for me and boom, it just started happening. . . . But I had other chicks that wanted to be in a committed relationship and I couldn't do it. Like I said, man . . . to answer your question, no. I think I had been perfectly happy being single.

Offering a slightly different perspective, Thomas was of the opinion that he has grown and evolved beyond the thinking that being in a relationship defines masculinity. In sharing this perspective, he alludes to the fact that society creates an expectation that men be involved in relationships and that when this is not the case, it leads to questions and possible skepticism about their masculinity.

> I actually feel that I've, perhaps, evolved to a place in manhood where I feel like I can exist as a fulfilled man without necessarily having marriage as a part of my life dynamic. I maybe in my younger days, perhaps I didn't feel like that . . . I've developed a stronger sense of self. Stronger sense of what, or let's say a broader perspective or a less confined perspective of what manhood and masculinity is. It doesn't necessarily mean being a strong man or a masculine man that you have to have a woman in your, or shall I say a wife as it relates to marriage, as a part of your life dynamic . . . I know societally, there are, I guess, questions that come up if a person obviously is male and has lived a good portion of their lives and has not been married or is an older male and is not married, there may be questions that may arise relative to that individual's masculinity and

manliness. What's wrong? Why you ain't married? You know, you a handsome man, where's your wife?

Finally, fatherhood, not involvement in a romantic relationship, was invoked as a defining feature of masculinity. Although some of the men felt as though it was their relationship or marriage that facilitated their involvement with their children, which in turn activated their sense of masculinity, others separated their identities as fathers from their identities as mates and men. Representative of these thoughts were Brian and Quincy. According to each of them, it was their choice to prioritize providing for and spending time with their children in promotion of their healthy growth and development that made them men rather than their participation in a romantic relationship. To be more specific, Brian stated:

> No. You don't have to be in a relationship to be a man. For instance, when I was not with anyone, it was just me and my daughter, I was a man. I was providing for her. I wasn't being a deadbeat dad. Regardless, I'm taking care of her not only with money but also with time and things like that. That's something that you want to do. You don't have to be in a relationship to know your role. You just got to take care of business basically.

Similarly, Quincy says that raising his children is what makes him a man, not being married or involved in a romantic relationship. He further argues that not only is his concept of masculinity not defined by his romantic relationships, but that in fact, it is the other way around. According to him, who he is as a man impacts his relationships.

> I don't know if it is. I know that who I am as a man influences my relationships. I don't know if it's the other way around. I don't know if me being a man, I have to be in a relationship or I have to act a certain way in a relationship. I think that's primarily due because of my idea of masculinity. Raising my son and my daughters, that's what makes me a man.

## CONCLUSION

In this chapter, whether or not the men felt as though their masculine identities were shaped by romantic relationships or marriages was explored. The findings revealed that 62.5 percent of the men agreed that their romantic relationships or marriages shaped their concepts of masculinity. In elaborating on this belief, the men discussed how being married or in a romantic relationship created opportunities for intimacy and companionship with their partners, encouraged them to be responsible as men and fathers, and reinforced traditional gender roles, all of which they saw as behavioral manifestations of manhood. The other 37.5 percent of the men rejected the idea that romantic relationships or marriages impacted their masculine identity. It should be noted that this opinion was expressed by men who were not involved in romantic relationships at the time they were interviewed, as well as men who were currently involved in committed relationships and marriages. According to these men, their manhood was defined by their self-reliance and independence and feeling liberated and secure enough in themselves to engage in a relationship or not if they saw fit. Interestingly, as some men argued that their concept of masculinity was influenced by their relationship creating a pathway for their fathering, and taking active roles in raising their children, other men rejected the salience of relationships in shaping masculinity but also invoked fatherhood. However, rather than making the case that their relationship facilitated their involvement, these men discussed prioritizing fathering over participation in a romantic relationship.

The findings here represent both an affirmation and an extension of the current research on black masculinity, the factors shaping it and the ways in which it is reflected in marriage or romantic relationships. On one hand, the men's narratives are consistent with the existing literature that for some of the men, particularly those rejecting that romantic relationships impacted their concept of masculinity, their masculinity was expressed through the significance that they placed on being independent, focused on personal development, and prioritizing fatherhood. Somewhat surprisingly, this perspective was expressed by men who were both single and romantically involved. Also consistent with previous research was the fact that many of the men subscribed to and espoused traditional gender role orientations that were evidenced by the manner in which they emphasized financial provision, patriarchal and heteronormative family structure, and a rejection of femininity. On the other hand, the men offered insight into some areas that have not been thoroughly examined in previous research with the potential to fill gaps in the existing literature on black masculinity. For example, the overwhelming majority of the men attested to the fact that their concept of masculinity was shaped by their romantic relationships. These men talked openly about how their desire for companionship was met through their connections to their romantic relationships. The men also edified and uplifted their intimate partners for helping to make them more accountable and responsible as men. That there were both older and younger men expressing this opinion represents a departure from current literature on black men that portrays them, particularly young black men, as predatory, hit-and-run mercenaries who are selfish and lack empathy. Given that most of the research on black masculinity is deficit framed and concludes that the meanings that black men ascribe to their masculine identity are shaped by economic disadvantage and racial discrimination, it is important to uplift a more diverse set of authentic black male voices, experiences, and perspectives to advance the state of knowledge. In doing so, future research can manifest Collins' (2004) call to unpack black gender ideology, redefine troublesome notions of masculinity, and enable black men to embrace the range of choices they actually have in becoming the kinds of men they want to be.

# Chapter Seven

# Reflections and Recaps

The purpose of *Black Love Matters* was to advance the state of knowledge in response to the dearth of academic literature on black male-female marriages and romantic relationships featuring firsthand authentic accounts and perspectives from black men. As Burton, Burton, and Austin (2016) explain, the voices of black men have been muted in the larger society such that they are largely visibly invisible. More specifically, according to Childs, Laudone, and Tavernier (2010), there is a paucity of empirical research about the attitudes of blacks concerning gender roles, dating practices, and attitudes toward marriage. Much of what we do know about dating, relationships, and marriage between black men and black women focuses on the relationships that are not occurring and the problems in relationships (Lawson and Thompson 1999). Moreover, we know even less about the experiences of middle-income black couples. In response, *Black Love Matters* set out to examine black male-female romantic relationships and marriages from the perspective of black men. The study followed a sample of 33 black men who were diverse with regard to age, marital status, educational attainment, and socioeconomic status. The study followed these men over the course of 4 years to trace their relationship trajectories and the micro and macro factors shaping them. Data analysis produced several emergent themes, the most salient of which were represented in *Black Love Matters'* chapters. These included the men's perspectives on the ways in which their sexual attitudes and behaviors, experiences with trauma, relationships transitions, and concepts of masculinity shaped and were shaped by their romantic relationships.

In chapter 3, "Let's Talk about Sex," the men discussed their willingness to engage in casual sex versus sex in committed relationships, sex and faithfulness, the influence of media, and connection between sex and intimacy. Close to one-third of the men expressed views suggesting that they were favorable to the idea of casual sex. Many of the men espousing this pro casual sex senti-ment were speaking from a historical, rather than contemporary perspective as many of these men were currently married or in a committed romantic relationship. However, many of these same men also discussed how what started out as casual sex led to one or both people "catching feelings" which led to the development of a relationship. For the men who rejected the no-tion of casual sex, they cited perceiving pre-marital sex as immoral, concerns about fathering children outside of a committed relationship or marriage and its implications for their ability to maintain an active role in their children's lives, and evolving to a point in their lives where they were interested in set-tling down with a stable partner. Closely related to the discussions of casual sex versus sex in the context of a romantic relationship was the issue of faith-fulness wherein the men shared that infidelity or the threat of it loomed large over many of their past or current relationships. The men also spoke candidly about the influence of media on their sexual attitudes and behaviors. When sharing their stories, the men talked about the prominent role of media and how it inundates them with messages about sex which they felt contributed to a culture encouraging casual sex and infidelity. There was also discussion about the ways in which black men are targeted by media and that their por-trayals are overly sexual. These feelings are consistent with previous research concluding that black bodies are stereotyped as hypersexual and promiscuous (Slatton and Plates 2016) contributing to a culture of mistrust that hurts rela-tionships between black men and women. Perhaps the most revealing finding in this chapter was that many of the men sought intimacy with their partners and wives and that they separated this sense of intimacy from sex. When do-ing so, the men stated their interest was to connect with their partners on a deeper-than-physical level. To do so, they often invoked Chapman's (2010) *Love Languages* and how they studied it to better understand their partners' innermost motivations and desires. That the men in the study emphasized achieving intimacy should not be overlooked because in many couples, sex is used as a primary means of intimacy. However, Shelton-Wheeler (2013) suggests that black couples need to identify additional meaningful ways to communicate their feelings and intentions toward each other. As the author also suggests, while sex can be a very healthy way of expressing affection, it can also become a distraction from the verbal communication that is neces-sary in relationships.

In chapter 4, "Trials, Tribulations, and Trauma," the men shared how their romantic relationships had been negatively impacted by previous exposure to various types of traumas. These included psychological trauma, physical trauma, and relationship trauma. Nearly 40 percent of the men reported hav-ing previous psychological trauma that included direct and indirect exposure to mental illness and substance abuse. In recounting these experiences, the men shared their concerns that the enduring legacy of slavery, community violence, as well as personal and familial tragedies led to emotional stress that made establishing and maintaining their relationships more difficult. Similarly, previous research has concluded that community based contextual factors influence relational schemas. According to Kogan et al. (2013), exposure to deviance in communities and racial discrimination can lead people to anticipate mistreatment from others in interpersonal relationships and contribute to a negative view of relationships. Such experiences can lead individuals to become defensive, guarded, and overly focused on self-reliance, making forging healthy relationships with romantic partners difficult. As for physical trauma, nearly one quarter of the men reported histories with child abuse, sexual abuse, and exposure to domestic violence. In sharing their stories, the men discussed how these experiences shaped their romantic relationship trajectories for years to come. The most notable examples were Josh and Dan. In Josh's case, he suffered abuse as a child, but later sought out women resembling his perpetrator and to exploit while Dan struggled with his sexual orientation for years after being assaulted as a child. The connection between the men's victimization and their relationship challenges drew parallels to Cassidy and Stevenson's (2005) study which concluded hyper vulnerability was associated with hyper masculine aggression among black males especially in the sense that both can be seen as a response to fear and sensitivity to rejection. In addition to the reports of psychological and physical trauma, the most frequently reported type of trauma was relationship trauma. Close to 70 percent of the men reported experiencing relationship trauma in past relationships. These traumas included infidelity, high conflict relationships, and the relationship inhibiting perspectives and behaviors of the men's families of origin, all of which resulted in an inability or extreme difficulty to trust. The fact that many of the men found it difficult to trust their subsequent partners after experiencing a relationship trauma is consistent with the notion of betrayal trauma which Owen, Quirk, and Manthos (2012) found to be negatively associated with the level of respect and trust that individuals had for their partners.

In chapter 5, "A Change Gonna Come," the men chronicled their relationship transitions and trajectories. Data analysis revealed that nearly half of the participants experienced at least one relationship transition during the 4-year study period. These transitions included men going from not being involved in a romantic relationship to having a serious girlfriend, men going from being divorced or single to being married, men going from being involved in a romantic relationship to breaking up and remaining single, and men being married but experiencing a separation during the study period. For men who went from not being involved in a romantic relationship to having a serious girlfriend, it was the juxtaposition between their former and current partners in terms of attitude and temperament that led to their receptivity to pursuing the new relationship. The men who went from being divorced or single to being married reported that finding a compatible partner and re-connecting with old friends with whom they felt safe increased their receptivity to marrying. The men who went from being in a relationship to being and remaining single over time cited difficult divorces and shifting priorities that did not include new relationships as their reasons for refraining from engaging new relationships. For the men who were married but experienced a separation during the study period, selfishness, as well as a lack of empathy and reciprocity were mentioned as defining features of the marriages that contributed to the separations. In many ways, the research literature was corroborated by the men's narratives. Consistent with the findings from Bethea and Allen (2013), who concluded that when couples are not confident that their relationship will be successful, the amount of effort and dedication they invest in it will be reduced. This is also often the case when couples do not have a clear vision for what relationship success should look like. This was particularly true in the cases of Thomas, who stated that he had no interest in marriage or a relationship, Alex, who was reluctant to talk about emotions; Adam, who prioritized his career in filmmaking; and Sean, who seemed pessimistic about the prospects of reconciling with this wife after separating. The remaining men whose relationships remained stable across the entire study period were all married. In discussing the factors facilitating the stability of their marriages, the men talked about the roles that shared values, connecting with a peer network that included other married men, and receiving support from a partner to make it through a challenging time that stressed, but did not fracture the relationship. Central to the stable marriages and the factors supporting them was the presence of trust. According to Shelton-Wheeler (2013), the ability to trust in someone's intention, and to feel that someone is being sincere is an important concept within the black community. Once the initial level of trust is established, each partner feels secure that the other will meet their needs. As the men attested, it was the development of trust in their partner that served as a catalyst reinforcing their commitment to their marriages that protected them from changes or transitions.

In chapter 6, "Love and Manhood," there was interest in exploring the men's perspectives on the extent to which they felt that being in a romantic relationship was central to their concept of masculinity. Sixty-two percent of the men in the study reported that being involved in a romantic relationship was important to their sense of manhood. For these men, being in a romantic relationship shaped their concept of masculinity by creating opportunities for companionship, providing venues for the men to be emotionally expressive, holding them accountable for being better fathers and partners, and establishing parameters for shaping manhood by reinforcing gender roles. The remaining 37 percent of the men rejected the notion that their sense of masculinity was associated with their engagement in romantic relationships. For these men, self-reliance, making a commitment to personal development, having the freedom and flexibility to make their own decisions, and behaving responsibly were all defining features of manhood.

The extant research literature provides some context for better understanding the men's perspectives. For example, several of the men disclosed that being in a romantic relationship impacted their concept of masculinity through its reinforcement of gender roles. In other words, for these men, being in a romantic relationship provided them with the opportunity to play their socially prescribed role which helped them feel like men. As Shelton-Wheeler (2013) found, couples tend to default to traditional gender roles modeled within Western society. The socialized roles specific to males are privileged and include men being the primary financial supporter and decision makers in the relationship. Contrarily, women tend to be socialized to defer to male authority and be the emotional caregivers in the relationship. This is consistent with the finding that many of the men stated that they favored a more egalitarian structure to their relationships when it came to a preference for dual earner households, yet they also expressed attitudes indicating that as men, they still wanted to preserve the decision making power. For example, William stated:

> In the past, the man was the primary breadwinner and had the fiscal responsibility for supporting the household. That's not true as much today. It's been somewhat, the female takes on as much responsibility or a greater responsibility in some respects. That's not how I grew up, and I'm still nothing like that. Although my wife was bringing in equal income, I still pretty much paid all the bills and took care of the financial support of the home, and then she would have specialized responsibilities like her car payment, her charges, and food, and stuff like that. Helping out with the educational stuff. The primary, the roof over the head, and these little emergencies, I've always taken that responsibility. . . . If you're in that marriage relationship, there's certain expectations that you're the head of the household to some degree. I think that's been watered-down lately, but still, in your household, everybody seems to hold you responsible. It's success or its failure. You're supposed to be the leader and protect our family and help set goals for the family. Culturally, that's been the role the man has played in the household. I still think it happens to some degree. If something goes wrong in a home, they point to the man, what about your policies? It was something you did, or wasn't doing, that contributed to it.

Here, William acknowledges that contemporarily, women often take on as much financial responsibility as men. In fact, he states that his wife was "bringing in equal income." However, he describes his role as "primary" and characterizes her financial contributions as "helping out" He also points to the social pressure placed on men when he talks about the idea that although both men and women contribute, when things go awry, people "point to the man."

Related to this, Shelton-Wheeler (2013) also suggests that economic stress can evoke negative emotions among black couples, resulting in resentment and marital dissatisfaction. Therefore, many black couples may find it difficult to operate within the traditional gender roles of the male being the primary breadwinner but instead may have to operate within a household where either or both partners take on that role. An example of this tension was Jeff who reported needing constant reassurance from his new wife that she was satisfied in the marriage and was not planning on leaving him when his business was struggling. Similarly, Keith shared that his family's financial challenges that were brought on by multiple layoffs contributed his increased stress level that he addressed by staying out late at night which eventually led to a separation.

Existing research also offers a number of possible explanations for the men reporting that their sense of masculinity was not shaped by their involvement in romantic relationships. Some of the men stating that being in a relationship was not central to their concept of being a man cited personal freedom and flexibility. Franklin's (2004) analysis revealed that it is common for men to feel that their women hold them back or stand in their way. Also, men tend to prioritize the protection of their dignity, while women place survival of the family first. Therefore, to listen to the lessons and directions of a female challenges some men's sense of leadership and potentially exposes men's failings and the insecurities. Representative of this thinking was Joe, who in response to being asked what he thought were some of the largest obstacles that black couples face, stated "It may be a stereotype or whatever, but just this idea that the women [black women] wants to run the household. But they have opinions too and you've got guys who . . . historically have not been not been able to handle that. They [the men] want to be *the* boss and so they want to run everything." This is also similar to Thomas who mentioned that he divorced in large part because of the fallout from his ex-wife questioning his authenticity and leadership and a result, he stated that he would rather be single and remained that way across the entire study period.

Although the existing literature emphasizes economics and decision making in its examinations of the ways in which romantic relationships do or do not shape men's sense of masculinity, the men in the study offered perspectives that provide new insights. For example, Chris talked about how his need for physical touch and intimacy could only be achieved in the context of a romantic relationship. Moreover, Keith shared that as a man, he was his most authentic self when he felt free to be emotionally expressive and he credited his wife with creating the space for him to do so. Some of the men who did not think that being in a romantic relationship shaped their concept of masculinity pointed to things such as raising their children as a single father or rising in the ranks of their chosen field or profession as having more impact on their sense of manhood than whether they were engaged in a romantic relationship. Interestingly, the men's response to whether being in a romantic relationship impacted their concept of masculinity was not dependent upon whether the men were actually in a relationship. In other words, there were men who were not involved with anyone who agreed that being in a romantic relationship was important to their concept of manhood and there were men who were romantically involved and married who were of the opinion that their relationship was not connected to their sense of manhood.

## ADVICE FROM THE STUDY PARTICIPANTS

Consistent with the notion of lifting up the voices of authentic black men to share their experiences and perspectives on romantic relationships and marriages, there was interest in soliciting the men's opinions on what they felt was important to share with other black men and women involved in romantic relationships. In doing so, the men offered their insights into a number of areas including advice related to mate selection, courtship and dating, as well as commitment and perseverance.

### Mate Selection

The first category of the men's advice was mate selection. In offering this advice, the men were primarily focused on sharing the types of traits and qualities that men and women should look for in potential partners. When sharing advice for men, the recommendations were simple and succinct. Examples of advice offered for black men included, "don't make babies with people you don't know," "get to know your partner," and find someone with whom you are "equally yoked." However, the advice to women was more detailed and substantive. Consider the quote below from Jeff:

> If I was talking to women, I would tell them find the nerdiest guy you can find and marry him. Because I think about a lot of our friends, now, they are single or they are single moms. No matter how educated they are, with good friends who have MBAs and law degrees. No husband, no girlfriend. I don't know what

it is . . . maybe that they waited too long. In terms of dealing with females, if you waited too long, those material guys who were looking, to me they were looking back in undergrad. They were following that trajectory of dating all those women to meet someone and so they really missed the action. Some of my wife's friends say, "Why can't I find a guy like you?" Well, because they already got married. . . . Yeah. I'm not saying that there aren't any out there, but the volume of them have already gotten married. You might catch them in their late 40s, after they divorced. By then, they are jaded and you don't want to.

Jeff's advice for black women is a call for them to look for the potential in intelligent and well-mannered black men. In his initial interviews, Jeff talked openly about the fact that until college, he did not have much experience with women. He stated that he was never the coolest, best looking, or most athletic guy and as a result, he did not date much until he connected with his now wife who he described as "gorgeous." However, because of his intellect, work ethic, and easy-going temperament, Jeff graduated from college and later started his own business. Over time, Jeff became successful which situates his wife in an advantageous financial position vis-à-vis most of her friends, particularly those who remain single. In response to them asking him about their prospects to find a "good man," Jeff mentions that much like himself, they [the good men] are already involved in relationships. In sum, Jeff is arguing that men like him who were not perceived as attractive potential partners early on should be given a chance before they are all married and spoken for.

On the other hand, Brian, a police detective, is much more assertive and traditional in his orientation. In addressing his advice to black women, he urges them to be with a, "fucking man." By this, Brian emphasizes what he feels are men's natural responsibilities which are providing for and protecting their families. And in exchange for this provision and protection, men were the unquestioned leaders and heads of their households.

> Okay. If you're going to be with a man . . . if I'm talking to a woman and I'm telling her how to be with a man, make sure he's a fucking man. Make sure he knows his role as a man. As I always say there's some people who, "Yeah I'm a man" and this and that, but they're showing they're not doing it. They're not living up to it. They're not being a man. A man is still considered the head of the household, he should be a man.

In both cases, Jeff and Brian's advice directly reflected their personal circumstances. In previous interviews, Jeff described himself as someone who was not very handsome and would never have a chance to date a "vixen" while Brian talked at length about gender roles and the importance of each person living up to the social script created for men and women by the larger society.

## Courtship and Dating

Another popular area for the men's advice was courtship and dating. Unlike with their advice on mate selection, the men did not separate their advice for men from that which they offered to women. Instead, they spoke broadly about what they felt would be good for broader black culture. In doing so, they placed a lot of emphasis on slowing down and not rushing into relationships. Interview excerpts from Rex and Dan were representative of these sentiments. First, Rex shares the ways in which taking things slowly can be helpful in establishing the type of solid foundation built on trust, communication, and a willingness to evolve with your partner that will allow for the relationship to be stable and sustainable.

> Take it slow in regards to getting to know the person. Take it step-by-step. I'll also say, Physically, sexually, take it slow, because sometimes that can be the underpinning reason of why some relationships continue when they shouldn't, because if they're being satisfied physically, I'd say take it slow there. I'd say definitely get to trust the person, and vice-versa, and to communicate regularly, communicate and being able to troubleshoot different problems that are going to come up. It's always a work in progress, and so that's something that I'd definitely share, and just be willing to give more than you receive. . . . People change and relationships change, so that you're going to have to adapt with that as the relationship grows is a given. I think that if folks have that understanding that it's not going to be that route that it was 5 years ago, 10 years ago, but it's a little bit different structure, and they continue to work with that, then I think that's how they're successful and sustainable.

In his quote, Rex is encouraging black men and women to be intentional about getting to know one another to facilitate the relationship's success and avoiding the potential pitfalls of becoming accustomed to the physical satisfaction that may come with having sex before other areas of the relationship are solidified. Dan also cautions black men and women against prematurely jumping into relationships, but he has a slightly different perspective. In the quote below, rather than taking things slowly to facilitate the relationship's success, he argues that not every interaction or date should lead to a relationship.

> In relationships, I think culturally, speaking of people of color, I think sometimes we try to force every situation into a relationship. Every person we meet, I see it all the time, we try to make them "the one," but it is okay to just date. It is okay to date. It is okay to go out with someone, go have dinner, make out. I don't think you should score all of them, and I think that's where black people struggle, but I think it's okay to date. It's okay to go out with somebody for a little bit, then go out with somebody else. Go out with Bob on Monday, another

guy on Friday, I don't see a big deal. Culturally, I see my white friends able to do that so much easier than my black friends. I think part of it is white people learn how to date. I really do. I remember growing up, my parents—nobody taught me how to date. You just kind of figure it out. It was, I was told don't be too serious about somebody and don't have sex, don't do this. It was all the don'ts, it was always a negative thing. It was never in the positive. My white friends, their parents encouraged them. I noticed with all of my black friends, because you wouldn't get that support, when you did bring somebody around, you wanted your parents to see how serious you were about them. You wanted them to understand what a good person they were, and sometimes you didn't want to take to meet you folks because you know, sometimes with black people, we think every person that we bring around—you don't want them to think that you're having sex with all of them.

Here, Dan shares that in his opinion, black people tend to force people into relationships before they are ready. He also draws a distinction between the way that he thinks black people and white people tend to approach the subject of dating. Much of this distinction is based on the taboo nature of sex in many black families. According to Dan, one reason why there is so much pressure to be in a "relationship" is because there is a sense among many that people are having sex with everyone that they date. Given some black people's interest in not being perceived as promiscuous, they either rush into or are forced into relationships prematurely. This phenomenon is reminiscent of the controlling images that Collins (2004) and Kniffley, Brown, and Davis (2018) discussed as they relate to the ways in which negative stereotypes about black people's sexuality create circumstances where they find themselves looking to refute racist misconceptions by opting to behave *respectably*. As the conversation continued, Dan went on to discuss his experience in dating a white woman who seemingly abruptly decided that she no longer wanted to date him because she concluded that someone else that she was concurrently dating was a better match. He recalls being torn between being upset and feeling refreshed as he stated:

I dated one white female in my life. We were cool, we were dating, we were intimate, but we had never had that conversation [about the exclusivity or lack thereof of their relationship]. When I go to the black women that I dated, it was understood, we together, whether we talk about it or not. With this white lady, one day she was like, "Well you know, I've been dating somebody else, I've been dating so-and-so, we decided that we're going through with it. This is getting more serious." Basically, she felt like she didn't want to date me anymore. I was like, "Word?" She was like "Yeah," and I felt like I should be mad, but I wasn't. She was like, "It was fun, it was cool, I enjoyed myself, thank you for being nice," yada, yada, yada, "but this is what I want to do." It was so refreshing, because I've always said that too many black people don't break up well. It has to be negative. Sometimes there's no catastrophic event, there's no bombs over Baghdad, sometimes it's just not fun anymore, it's not something you want to do. Black people, we like to have that event, we like to have that drama. We want to bomb something, catch something, be something over the top. It's not just in relationships. It's with jobs, it's with church situations. I've seen so many people that have to be negative in order for them to make the change. Sometimes it's not bad, but it still needs to change, and it's okay.

In sharing this experience, Dan illustrates a point made by Lawson and Thompson (1999) when they argued that one of the challenges to black male-female relationships has been that dating has not been a structured process used to assess potential mates. Rather, historically, it has been what they called a catch-as-catch-can matter. Making matters worse is the reality that while black men and women used to meet in school, churches, and in the neighborhood, their increased mobility means that these opportunities have decreased over time. The result is that increasingly, contemporary couples have limited knowledge of their partner's character in these settings where family and friends used to be positioned to bring attention to signs of incompatibility.

## Commitment and Perseverance

The final area that the men addressed in their advice revolved around commitment and perseverance. When sharing advice in this category, the men were providing practical tips and strategies that black men and women could put into practice to strengthen their relationships.

For example, Jake mentioned that people needed to simply "choose to love your mate versus not choosing to love them." Several men also talked about the importance of the limiting the number of people who had access to information about their relationship or as Robert said, "keep people out of your business." Wayne shared similar advice when he stated:

> I think the most thing that people need to know is to, if you decide to get married, just experience it for yourself and not listen to anybody else's advice on what happens in marriage. I think you should just develop your marriage the way you all want it to happen and not be exposed to somebody's negative criticism or whatever else. I think that can definitely affect the way you think and view marriage before you even get into it.

That Wayne would encourage others to refrain from listening to the opinions of naysayers or critics was not surprising. Recall that in his initial interview, he was reluctant to pursue a romantic relationship because he had recently broken up with a longtime girlfriend and had witnessed many of his family members go through divorce. However, he later re-connected with an old friend who he would eventually marry, so it stands to reason that he would push back against being influenced by people external to the relationship. In addition to limiting the number of people providing input on the relationship, many other men offered advice about how to either avoid or resolve conflict. In these instances, the men talked a lot about the importance of patience and communication. They also talked about being willing to listen and to put yourself in your partner's shoes to better understand their perspective. As was discussed in chapter 5, having shared core values was also cited as critical to effective conflict resolution from the standpoint that even when couples disagreed, having similar core values meant that there would likely be some consensus on how to agree to disagree without there being lingering negative effects. In some cases, shared core values were linked to religious beliefs, such as when Adam stated, "commitment goes back to the spiritual side. For me, if you're tied together with God, you can get through it all." Yet in other cases, cores values were not associated with religion or spirituality as evidenced by in the following quote from Anthony.

> Honesty, respect, and understanding. You got to be honest. If something happens, let the other person know, let them know how you feel, don't hold back, stuff like that. Don't hold no grudge, that's the worst thing, you never hold a grudge. If you're mad about something, let it be known because you've got to talk it out.

Finally, there was Keith who like many of the other men, provided advice that was in direct response to his relationship trajectory. In chapter 5, Keith revealed that he and his wife separated for a period of 6 months. Keith admitted that he had been taking his wife for granted but that she got his attention when she left their home to go back to live with her mother. It was at this time, that he began "sweating" her by going to his mother-in-law's home to visit in an attempt to convince his wife that he was serious about changing his behavior. In his final follow up interview, he shares a story about his grandfather and credits him with establishing a standard for dedication and commitment that helped him save his marriage.

> It's a old one but I just keep hearing him [grandfather] say. You've got to be built Ford tough. First you've got to be built to make it last. You've got to look at it like every mistake that somebody makes is not designed for divorce. It may be some infidelity in some relationships, it may be financial situations in some relationships, whatever the case may be, but the first thing is not divorce. You've got to sit down and you've got to reconcile it and you've got to go through it. Me being separated for the six or seven months, I would just look for my grandfather and I would always listen to exactly what he said. Either you're

going to be built Ford tough or you going to be a . . . he said you're going to be a bitch. That's the way he talked. I was just like, "You know granddaddy I'm built Ford tough." And he was like, "Well that's the way we roll in this family."

As Keith's quote illustrates, despite the challenges, he remained dedicated to working through his problems with his wife. As such, his advice to other black men and women was to "sit down and reconcile" when faced with relationship problems because in his opinion, "the first thing is not divorce." This thinking was consistent with that of many of the other men who also felt that it was important for black men and women to remain committed to their relationships instead of breaking up at the first sign of trouble.

## RECOMMENDATIONS AND CONCLUSIONS

Much of the available demographic data indicates that black male-female relationships are plagued by low marriage rates and high levels of conflict and discord. However, Karenga (2014) argues that black male-female relationships are no more pathological than other groups' male-female relationships. Moreover, any discussion of problems has to be contextualized against a backdrop of the deleterious combination of capitalism, racism, and sexism conspiring to create the structural inequality that disadvantages black men and women, creating additional strain on their relationships. As such, any critique of black male-female relationships should also include a critique of the broader society for its role in creating the conditions shaping these relationships. It should also be noted that not all black male-female romantic relationships are in turmoil, as evidenced by the fact that nearly half of the study participants' relationships remained stable across the 4-year data collection period. Nevertheless, completely avoiding relationship problems is unrealistic. Therefore, what's more important is exploring what can be done to assist black men and women in being resourceful in developing solutions to their relationship challenges (Wanzo 2011). To this end, the concluding section contains recommendations for practitioners working with black couples that are compiled from the research literature and the lived experiences of the men in the study.

### Recommendation 1: Acknowledge the injurious effect of racism, capitalism, and patriarchy

According to Karenga (2014), examinations of the major challenges facing black male-female relationships are rooted in structural rather than individual causes. Therefore, in order to better understand our relationships, we must first understand the contexts that shape them. Here in the U.S., those contexts are heavily influenced by capitalism, racism, and sexism. Capitalism turns relationships into commodities. Racism contributes to self-hate, self-doubt, and pathological preoccupation on a white paradigm. Sexism encourages men to pursue artificial personal power over women as a substitute for real social power over one's destiny and daily life. Therefore, we must acknowledge the insidious nature of these -isms and recognize their negative impacts on black male-female romantic relationships and marriages. In doing so, as Lee (2016) calls for, we can stop asking, "what's wrong with you?" and start asking more humanizing questions such as, "what happened to you?"

## Recommendation 2: Identity work

In addition to acknowledging the negative impacts that capitalism, racism, and sexism have had on black male-female romantic relationships, identity exploration is also recommended. Previous research suggests that a strong racial identity among black people serves as a protective factor against environmental and psychological stress (Sullivan and Esmail 2012), therefore gathering information about a couple's racial identity is an important assessment tool. Clinicians can facilitate discussions with couples related to their cultural values, roles, attitudes, cultural stressors, and connectedness to the black community. In doing so, practitioners can obtain important information concerning ethnic identity, gender identity, and cultural values of the men and women they serve. Subsequently, as Allen and Helm (2013) suggest, black men and women can then reconcile the socialization processes that promote self-reliance, independence, and toughness in women and the so-called protective cool-pose defense mechanism often exhibited by men with the importance of compromise and interdependence. In doing so, perhaps more black male-female relationships will be characterized by cooperation as opposed to competition.

## Recommendation 3: Reexamine socialization patterns around dating

Many of the men in the study discussed how their relationship schemas were influenced by their families of origin. Therefore, we know that familial and fictive kin networks play an important role in socializing youth around dating and relationships. Although several men talked about receiving positive socialization from relationship role models that they had access to growing up, many of them lamented the fact that those around them provided examples that made them reluctant and apprehensive about romantic relationships. Studies involving black youth have also concluded that large numbers of black males reported exposure to male role models inside and outside of the home who regularly devalued women (Peters et al. 2010). Further, teen romantic relationships often serve as the training ground for the romantic relationships adolescents may experience later as adults. If a teenager experiences negative dating relationships (e.g., chronic conflict and disappointment or abuse), they may develop a negative outlook on the benefits of adult relationships and marriage (Simons et al. 2012).To combat this problematic socialization, it is recommended that practitioners integrate parents, caregivers, and mentors into intervention and prevention efforts to reshape how black youth perceive romantic relationships (Hurt et al. 2014) so that into the future, larger numbers of black men and women will feel loved and enhanced in their relationships rather than threatened by them.

## CONCLUSION

In sum, given how often black men have been implicated in discussions about what ails their romantic relationships and marriages, it stands to reason that their voices should be prominent in discussions aimed at better understanding these relationships and discussions centering on potential solutions (Hurt et al. 2014). To that end, *Black Love Matters* represents an important step forward in research on black men and their romantic relationships and marriages as it uplifts the authentic voices of a group of diverse black men spanning the intersectional spectrums. *Black Love Matters'* findings, as well as the conclusions drawn from them provide a unique building block that simultaneously fills a gap in the existing literature and sets the stage for further analysis. To continue to advance the state of knowledge in this area, future research should seek to triangulate black men's narratives with those of their partners. Future research should also be more explicit in its exploration of black male sexuality. Although all of the men enrolled in the study originally self-identified as heterosexual, over the course of the various data collection waves, it was revealed that at least one participant was secretly struggling with his sexuality. As we have seen in other research, to the extent that many men define masculinity using heterosexuality, both their conceptualizations of masculinity and sexuality play salient roles in their performance of each other, including their attitudes and behavior in romantic relationships and marriages (Bucher 2014). Future research should also embrace the notion that marriage may no longer be seen as the ultimate in romantic relationships (Allen and Helm 2013). If this is indeed the case, research should explore the possibility that there is a need for new models of healthy, fulfilling non-marital relationships that may not be defined by rings and licenses, but are nevertheless characterized by trust, commitment, and intimacy. Most importantly, future research should strive to reject the all-too-common deficit framed depictions of black romantic relationships as deviant and inferior in favor of a new narrative that compels researchers, practitioners, policymakers, public discourse, and popular culture to respect and celebrate the depth and diversity of those relationships.

# Bibliography

ABC News. 2009. "Excerpt: 'Act Like a Lady, Think Like a Man.'" April 12, 2009. https://abcnews.go.com/GMA/Books/steve-harvey-questions-woman-deep/story?id=9925391

Ajzen, Icek. *Attitudes, Personality, and Behavior. Milton-Keynes*, Maidenhead, Berkshire: Open. 1988.

Ajzen, Icek. "From Intentions to Actions: A Theory of Planned Behavior." In *Action control*, edited by Julius Kuhl and Jurgen Beckmann. Berlin: Springer, 1985, 11–39.

Ajzen, Icek. "The Theory of Planned Behavior." *Organizational Behavior and Human Decision Processes* 50, no. 2 (1991): 179–211.

Allen, Tennille, and Katherine Helm. "Threats to Intimacy for African American Couples." In *Love, Intimacy, and the African American Couple*, edited by Katherine M. Helm and Jon Carlson. New York: Routledge. 2013, 85–116.

Anderson, Edward R., and Shannon M. Greene. "Transitions in Parental Repartnering After Divorce." *Journal of Divorce & Remarriage* 43, no. 3–4 (2005): 47–62.

Anderson, Elijah. "Sex Codes and Family Life Among Northon's Youth." In *Streetwise: Race, Class, and Change in an Urban Community*, edited by Elijah Anderson. Chicago: University of Chicago Press, 1990, 112–137.

Anne Braden Institute. "A Self-Guided Tour of Louisville's Civil Rights History." Louisville, KY: University of Louisville, KY. n.d.

Aubespin, Mervin, Kenneth Clay, and J. Blaine Hudson. *Two Centuries of Black Louisville: A Photographic History*. Louisville, KY: Butler Books, 2011.

Aymer, Samuel R. "'I Can't Breathe': A Case Study—Helping Black Men Cope with Race related Trauma Stemming from Police Killing and Brutality." *Journal of Human Behavior in the Social Environment* 26, no. 3–4 (2016): 367–376.

Backman, Melvin. 2017. "The Autobiography of Gucci Mane" and the Struggle to be Seen." *The New Yorker*, November 17, 2017. https://www.newyorker.com/books/page-turner/the autobiography-of-gucci-mane-and-the-struggle-to-be-seen.

Banks, Ralph Richard. *Is Marriage for White People?: How the African American Marriage Decline Affects Everyone.* New York: Plume, 2012.

Barker, Andrew. 2017. "Jay-Z's 4:44." *Variety,* June 30, 2017. https://variety.com /2017/music/news/album-review-jay-z-444-1202484062/.

Barr, Ashley B., Tara E. Sutton, Leslie Gordon Simons, K. A. S. Wickrama, and Frederick O. Lorenz. "Romantic Relationship Transitions and Changes in Health Among Rural, White Young Adults." *Journal of Family Psychology* 30, no. 7 (2016): 832.

Bell, Derrick. "The Sexual Diversion: The Black Man/Black Woman Debate in Context." In *Black Men on Race, Gender, and Sexuality: A Critical Reader,* edited by Devon W. Carbado New York: New York University Press. 1999, 237–248.

Bell, Yvonne R., Cathy L. Bouie, and Joseph A. Baldwin. "Afrocentric Cultural Consciousness and African-American Male-Female Relationships." *Journal of Black Studies* 21, no. 2 (1990): 162–189.

Benjamin, Lois. "The Dog Theory: Black Male-Female Conflict." In *African American Male-Female Relationships: A Reader*, edited by Patricia Dixon. San Diego, CA: Cognella Publishing, 2014, 53–62.

Bergdall, Anna R., Joan Marie Kraft, Karen Andes, Marion Carter, Kendra Hatfield-Timajchy, and Linda Hock-Long. "Love and Hooking Up in the New Millennium: Communication Technology and Relationships among Urban African American and Puerto Rican Young Adults." *Journal of Sex Research* 49, no. 6 (2012): 570–582.

Bethea, Sharon, and Tennille Allen. "Past and Present Societal Influences on African American Couples that Impact Love and Intimacy." In *Love, Intimacy, and the African American Couple,* edited by Katherine M. Helm and Jon Carlson. New York: Routledge. 2013, 20–59.

Blackman, Lorraine, Obie Clayton, Norval Glenn, Linda Malone-Colon, and Alex Roberts. "The Consequences of Marriage for African Americans: A Comprehensive Literature Review." New York, NY: *Institute for American Values* 54 (2005).

Blakeley, Craig, and Bertis Little. "The State of Black Louisville: The Health Perspective." In *State of Black Louisville.* Louisville, KY: Louisville Urban League. 2018, 105–107.

Brooms, Derrick R., Jelisa Clark, and Matthew Smith. "Being and Becoming Men of Character: Exploring Latino and Black males' Brotherhood and Masculinity through Leadership in College." *Journal of Hispanic Higher Education* 17, no. 4 (2018): 317–331.

Brooms, Derrick R., and Armon R. Perry. ""It's Simply Because We're Black Men" Black Men's Experiences and Responses to the Killing of Black Men." *The Journal of Men's Studies* 24, no. 2 (2016): 166–184.

Brown, Susan L. "Union Transitions among Cohabitors: The Significance of Relationship Assessments and Expectations." *Journal of Marriage and Family* 62, no. 3 (2000): 833–846.

Bucher, Jacob. "'But He Can't Be Gay': The Relationship between Masculinity and Homophobia in Father-Son Relationships." *The Journal of Men's studies* 22, no. 3 (2014): 222–237.

Burton, Linda, Dorian Burton, and Bobby Austin. "Repairing the Breach Revisited: A Focus on Families and Black Males." In *Boys and Men in African American Families*, edited by Linda Burton, Dorian Burton, Susan M. McHale, Valarie King, and Jennifer Van Hook. Cham, Switzerland: Springer International Publishing. 2016, 1–3.

Busby, Dean M., Eric C. Walker, and Thomas B. Holman. "The Association of Childhood Trauma with Perceptions of Self and the Partner in Adult Romantic Relationships." *Personal Relationships* 18, no. 4 (2011): 547–561.

Carroll, Jeff. 2011. "Book Review: Act Like a Lady, Think Like a Man." *Real Health,* April 20, 2011 https://www.realhealthmag.com/blog/book-review-act-like-a-lady-th

Cassidy, Elaine F., and Howard C. Stevenson Jr. "They Wear the Mask: Hypervulnerability and Hypermasculine Aggression among African American Males in an Urban Remedial Disciplinary School." *Journal of Aggression, Maltreatment & Trauma* 11, no. 4 (2005): 53–74.

Cazenave, Noel A., and Rita Smith. "Gender Differences in the Perception of Black Male-Female Relationships and Stereotypes." In *Black Families*, edited by Harold Cheatam and James B. Stewart. New York: Routledge, 2017, 149–170.

Chapman, G. *The Five Love Languages: The Secret to Love that Lasts*. Chicago: Northfield Chores. 2010.

Childs, E. C., Laudone, S., & Tavernier, L. 2010. "Revisiting Black Sexualities in Families: Problems, Puzzles, and Prospects." In *Black sexualities: Probing Powers, Passions, Practices, and Policies,* edited by Juan Battle and Sandra L. Barnes Piscatatway, NJ: Rutgers University Press, 2010, 138–154.

Chipperfield, Judith G., and Betty Havens. "Gender Differences in the Relationship Between Marital Status Transitions and Life Satisfaction in Later Life." *The Journals of Gerontology Series B: Psychological Sciences and Social Sciences* 56, no. 3 (2001): 176–186.

Chung, Man Cheung, and Laura J. Hunt. "Posttraumatic stress Symptoms and Well-being Following Relationship Dissolution: Past Trauma, Alexithymia, Suppression." *Psychiatric Quarterly* 85, no. 2 (2014): 155–176.

Cohen, Philip N., and Joanna R. Pepin. "Unequal Marriage Markets: Sex Ratios and First Marriage among Black and White Women." *Socius* 4, 2018.

Collins, Patricia Hill. *Black Feminist Thought: Knowledge, Consciousness, and the Politics of Empowerment*. New York: Routledge, 2002.

Collins, Patricia Hill. *Black Sexual Politics: African Americans, Gender, and the New Racism*. New York: Routledge, 2004.

Corbin, Juliet, and Anselm Strauss. *Basics of qualitative research: Techniques and procedures for developing grounded theory*. Thousand Oaks, CA: Sage Publications, 2014.

Creswell, John. *Qualitative Inquiry & Research Design: Choosing among Five Approaches*. Thousand Oaks, CA: Sage Publications, 2007.

Crook, Tylon, Chippewa M. Thomas, and Debra C. Cobia. "Masculinity and Sexuality: Impact on Intimate Relationships of African American Men." *The Family Journal* 17, no. 4 (2009): 360–366.

Dailey, René M., Andrea A. McCracken, Borae Jin, Kelly R. Rossetto, and Erik W. Green. "Negotiating Breakups and Renewals: Types of On-again/off-again Dating Relationships." *Western Journal of Communication* 77, no. 4 (2013): 382–410.

Dawson-Edwards, Cherie. "Disrupting Louisville's School-to-Prison Pipeline Through Restorative Justice." In *State of Black Louisville.* Louisville, KY: Louisville Urban League. 2018, 51–53.

DeGruy, Joy. (2005). *Post Traumatic Slave Syndrome: America's Legacy of Enduring Injury and Healing.* Milwaukie, Oregon: Uptone Press, 2005.

Dixon, Patricia. "Marriage among African Americans: What Does the Research Reveal?" In *African American Male-Female Relationships: A Reader,* edited by Patricia Dixon. San Diego, CA: Cognella Publishing. 2014, 287–301.

Edin, Kathryn, and Maria Kefalas. (2005). *Promises I Can Keep: Why Poor Women Put Motherhood Before Marriage.* Berkeley: University of California Press. 2005.

Felitti, Vincent, Robert Anda, Dale Nordenberg, David Williamson, Alison Spitz, Valarie Edwards, Mary Koss, and James Marks. "Relationship of Childhood Abuse and Household Dysfunction to Many of the Leading Causes of Death in Adults: The Adverse Childhood Experiences (ACE) Study." *American Journal of Preventive Medicine* 14, no 4 (1998): 245–258.

Fishbein, Martin and Icek Ajzen. *Belief, Attitude, Intention, and Behavior: An Introduction to Theory and Research.* Reading, MA: Addison-Wesley 1975.

Fishbein, Martin Ed. *Readings in Attitude Theory and Measurement.* Hoboken, NJ: Wiley. 1967.

Franklin, Anderson J. *From Brotherhood to Manhood.* Hoboken, NJ: Wiley, 2004.

Franklin, Clyde, and Walter Pillow. "Single and Married: The Black Male's Acceptance of the Prince Charming Ideal." In *African American Male-Female Relationships: A Reader,* edited by Patricia Dixon. San Diego, CA: Cognella Publishing. 2014, 17–24.

Gammage, Marquita Marie. *Representations of Black Women in the Media: The Damnation of Black Womanhood.* New York: Routledge, 2015.

Gerlach, Tanja M., Ruben C. Arslan, Thomas Schultze, Selina K. Reinhard, and Lars Penke. "Predictive Validity and Adjustment of Ideal Partner Preferences Across the Transition into Romantic Relationships." *Journal of Personality and Social Psychology* 116, no. 2 (2019): 313.

Goodwill, Janelle R., Nkemka Anyiwo, Ed-Dee G. Williams, Natasha C. Johnson, Jacqueline S. Mattis, and Daphne C. Watkins. "Media Representations of Popular Culture Figures and the Construction of Black Masculinities." *Psychology of Men & Masculinity* 20, no 3 (2019): 288–298.

Green, Adrienne. 2015. "Straight Outta Compton and the Social Burdens of Hip-Hop." *The Atlantic*, August 14, 2015. https://www.theatlantic.com/entertainment/archive/2015/08/straight-outta-compton-nwa/401279/.

Haldane, Eva C., Ronald B. Mincy, and Daniel P. Miller. "Racial Disparities in Men's Health and the Transition to Marriage among Unmarried Fathers." *Journal of Family Issues* 31, no. 9 (2010): 1183–1210.

Halford, Macy. 2009. "Best-Seller Bizzare: Steve Harvey's 'Act Like A Lady, Think Like a Man' is Still No. 1." March 27, 2009. https://www.newyorker.com/books/

page-turner/best-seller-bizarre-steve-harveys-act-like-a-lady-think-like-a-man-is-still-no-1

Halpern-Meekin, Sarah, and Laura Tach. "Discordance in Couples' Reporting of Courtship Stages: Implications for Measurement and Marital Quality." *Social Science Research* 42, no. 4 (2013): 1143–1155.

Hammersmith, Anna M. "Life Interrupted: Parents' Positivity and Negativity Toward Children Following Children's and Parents' Transitions Later in Life." *The Gerontologist* 59, no. 3 (2019): 519–527.

Hammond, Wizdom Powell. "Taking it Like a Man: Masculine Role Norms as Moderators of the Racial Discrimination–Depressive Symptoms Association among African American Men." *American Journal of Public Health* 102, no. 2 (2012): 232–241.

Harris III, Frank, Robert T. Palmer, and Laura E. Struve. "'Cool Posing' on Campus: A Qualitative Study of Masculinities and Gender Expression among Black Men at a Private Research Institution." *The Journal of Negro Education* (2011): 47–62.

Harvey, Steve. *Act Like a Lady, Think Like a Man: What Men Really Think about Love, Relationships, Intimacy, and Commitment.* New York: Harper Collins, 2009.

Hawkins, Stephanie. "Programs and Services for Black Male Survivors of Community Violence: What's Effective?" *Journal of Child & Adolescent Trauma* 10, no. 2 (2017): 139–145.

Henderson, Odie. 2013. "The Best Man Holiday." RogerEbert.com, November 14, 2013. https://www.rogerebert.com/reviews/the-best-man-holiday-2013

Herman, Judith. *Trauma and Recovery: The Aftermath of Violence from Domestic Abuse to Political Terror.* New York: Basic Books, 1992.

Hooks, Bell. *We Real Cool: Black Men and Masculinity.* New York: Routledge, 2004.

Hopkinson, Natalie, and Natalie Y. Moore. *Deconstructing Tyrone: A New Look at Black Masculinity in the Hip-Hop Generation.* Jersey City, NJ: Cleis Press, 2006.

Hurt, Tera R. "Black Men and the Decision to Marry." *Marriage & Family Review* 50, no. 6 (2014): 447–479.

Hurt, Tera R., Stacey E. McElroy, Kameron J. Sheats, Antoinette M. Landor, and Chalandra M. Bryant. "Married Black Men's Opinions as to why Black Women are Disproportionately Single: A Qualitative Study." *Personal Relationships* 21, no. 1 (2014): 88–109.

Hurt, Tera R., Jeffrey K. Shears, Margaret C. O'Connor, and Sharon B. Hodge. "Married Black Men's Observations of Fathers' Teachings about Husbandhood." *Personal Relationships* 24, no. 1 (2017): 84–101.

Hurt, Tera. R. "Toward a Deeper Understanding of the Meaning of Marriage among Black Men." *Journal of Family Issues*, 33, (2012): 1–26.

Jackson, Dana, and Jennie Jean Davidson. "Standing in the Gap: 15,000 Degrees Addresses the Opportunity Gap." In *State of Black Louisville.* Louisville, KY: Louisville Urban League. 2018, 72–74.

Jackson, Nikki R. "The Racial Wealth Gap: Addressing the Reasons and Possible Solutions." In *State of Black Louisville.* Louisville, KY: Louisville Urban League. 2018, 24–26.

Jenkins, Esther J., Edward Wang, and Larry Turner. "Traumatic Events Involving Friends and Family Members in a Sample of African American Early Adolescents." *American Journal of Orthopsychiatry* 79, no. 3 (2009): 398–406.

Jewell, Sue. "Black Male-Female Conflict: Internalization of Negative Definitions. Transmitted Through Imagery." In *African American Male-Female Relationships: A Reader*, edited by Patricia Dixon. San Diego, CA: Cognella Publishing. 2014, 37–46.

Jones, D. Marvin. *Race, Sex, and Suspicion: The Myth of the Black Male*. Santa Barbara, CA: Greenwood Publishing Group, 2005.

Jones, Johnny. "Narrative Blackness in the Great American Cable Television Drama." In *HBO's Treme and Post-Katrina Catharsis*, edited by Dominique Gendrin, Catherine Dessinges, and Shearon Roberts. Lanham, MD: Lexington Books. 2016, 257–286.

Jordan, Eric, and Derrick Brooms. "Black and Blue: Analyzing and Queering Black-Masculinities in Moonlight." In *Living Racism: Through the Barrel of the Book*, edited by Theresa Rajack-Talley and Derrick Brooms Lanham, MD: Lexington Books. 2017, 137–156.

Josefsson, Kim, Marko Elovainio, Sari Stenholm, Ichiro Kawachi, Maarit Kauppi, Ville Aalto, Mika Kivimäki, and Jussi Vahtera. "Relationship Transitions and Change in Health Behavior: A Four-phase, Twelve-year Longitudinal Study." *Social Science & Medicine* 209 (2018): 152–159.

Karenga, Maulana. "The Black Male-Female Connection." In *African American Male-Female Relationships: A Reader*, edited by Patricia Dixon. San Diego, CA: Cognella Publishing. 2014, 47–52.

Kniffley Jr, Steven, Bryan Davis, and Ernest Brown Jr. *Out of KOS (Knowledge of Self): Black Masculinity, Psychopathology, and Treatment*. New York: Peter Lang Publishers, 2018.

Kogan, Steven M., Man-Kit Lei, Christina R. Grange, Ronald L. Simons, Gene H. Brody, Frederick X. Gibbons, and Yi-fu Chen. "The Contribution of Community and Family Contexts to African American Young Adults' Romantic Relationship Health: A Prospective Analysis." *Journal of Youth and Adolescence* 42, no. 6 (2013): 878–890.

Kogan, Steven M., Tianyi Yu, and Geoffrey L. Brown. "Romantic Relationship Commitment Behavior among Emerging Adult African American Men." *Journal of Marriage and Family* 78, no. 4 (2016): 996–1012.

Kopotsha, Jazmin. 2017. "Everyone's Finally Watching 'Power' on Netflix. You'll Probably Want to too." Grazia, September 9, 2017. https://graziadaily.co.uk/life/tv-and-film/power-netflix-review/

Langlais, Michael R., Jacqueline S. DeAnda, Edward R. Anderson, and Shannon M. Greene."The Impact of Mothers' Post-Divorce Dating Breakups on Children's Problem Behaviors." *Journal of Child and Family Studies* 27, no. 8 (2018): 2643–2655.

Lang, Nico. 2012. "Think Like a Man Isn't Just Sexist: It's Offensive to Pretty Much-Everyone." *Huffington Post*, April 26, 2012. https://www.huffpost.com/entry/think-like-a-man-is-offensive_b_1449409

Lawrence-Webb, Claudia, Melissa Littlefield, and Joshua Okundaye. "African American Intergender Relationships: A Theoretical Exploration of Roles, Patriarchy, and Love." In *African American Male-Female Relationships: A Reader,* edited by Patricia Dixon. San Diego, CA: Cognella Publishing. 2014, 25–36

Lawson, Erma, and Aaron Thompson. *Black Men and Divorce.* Thousand Oaks, CA: Sage Publications. 1999.

Lee, Jocelyn R. S. "A Trauma Informed Approach to Affirming the Humanity of African American Boys and Supporting Healthy Transitions to Manhood." In *Boys and Men in African American Families,* edited by Linda M. Burton, Dorian Burton, Susan McHale, Valarie King, and Jennifer Van Hook. Cham, Switzerland: Springer International Publishing. 2016, 85–92.

Lichter, Daniel T., Zhenchao Qian, and Leanna M. Mellott. "Marriage or Dissolution? Union Transitions among Poor Cohabiting Women." *Demography* 43, no. 2 (2006): 223–240.

Lincoln, Karen D., Robert Joseph Taylor, and James S. Jackson. "Romantic Relationships among Unmarried African Americans and Caribbean Blacks: Findings from the National Survey of American Life." *Family relations* 57, no. 2 (2008): 254–266.

Luciano, Eva C., and Ulrich Orth. "Transitions in Romantic Relationships and Development of Self-esteem." *Journal of Personality and Social Psychology* 112, no. 2 (2017): 307.

Majors, Richard, and Janet Mancini Billson. *Cool Pose: The Dilemma of Black Manhood in America.* New York: Simon and Schuster, 1992.

Malton, Jordanna. "Creating Public Fictions: The Black Man as Producer and Consumer." *The Black Scholar* 40, no. 3 (2010): 36–42.

Marks, Loren D., Katrina Hopkins, Cassandra Chaney, Pamela A. Monroe, Olena Nesteruk, and Diane D. Sasser. "'Together, We are Strong': A Qualitative Study of Happy, Enduring African American Marriages." *Family Relations* 57, no. 2 (2008): 172–185.

Marks, Loren, Katrina Hopkins-Williams, Cassandra Chaney, Olena Nesteruk, and Diane Sasser. "My Kids and Wife Have Been My Life: Married African American Fathers Staying the Course." In *The Myth of the Missing Black Father*, edited by Roberta Coles and Charles Green. New York: Columbia University Press. 2010, 19–46.

May, Reuben A. Buford. *Talking at Trena's: Everyday Conversations at an African American Tavern.* New York: New York University Press, 2001.

McGruder, Kevin. "Pathologizing Black Sexuality: The U.S. Experience." In *Black Sexualities: Probing Powers, Passions, Practices, and Policies*, edited by Juan Battle and Sandra L. Barnes. Piscatatway, NJ: Rutgers University Press. 2010, 101–118.

Mincey, Krista, Moya Alfonso, Amy Hackney, and John Luque. "The Influence of Masculinity on Coping in Undergraduate Black Men." *The Journal of Men's Studies* 23, no. 3 (2015): 315–330.

Mitchell, Finesse. "What Black Men Wish Black Women Knew (But Don't Tell Them)." *Essence, 38,* no. 3 (2007): 114–116.

Montano, Daniel, and Danuta Kasprzyk. "Theory of Reasoned Action: Theory of Planned Behavior, and the Integrated Behavioral Model." In *Health Behavior and Health Education: Theory, Research, and Practice* edited by Karen Glanz, Barbara K. Rimer, and K. Viswanath. San Francisco, CA: John Wiley, 2008, 67–96.

Montemurro, Beth. "Getting Married, Breaking Up, and Making Up for Lost Time: Relationship Transitions as Turning Points in Women's Sexuality." *Journal of Contemporary Ethnography* 43, no. 1 (2014): 64–93.

Motley, Robert, and Andrae Banks. "Black Males, Trauma, and Mental Health Service Use: A Systematic Review." *Perspectives on Social Work: The Journal of the Doctoral Students of the University of Houston Graduate School of Social Work* 14, no. 1 (2018): 4.

National Association of Social Workers. "Code of Ethics of the National Association of Social Workers." Washington, DC: Author. 2017.

National Coalition Against Domestic Violence. "Domestic violence national statistics." Denver, CO: Author. 2015.

Neal, Mark Anthony. *New Black Man.* New York: Routledge, 2015.

Owen, Jesse, Kelley Quirk, and Megan Manthos. "I Get No Respect: The Relationship Between Betrayal Trauma and Romantic Relationship Functioning." *Journal of Trauma & Dissociation* 13, no. 2 (2012): 175–189.

Perry, Armon. "Fatherhood in Black Louisville: Challenges and Resources Impacting Paternal Involvement." In *State of Black Louisville.* Louisville, KY: Louisville Urban League. 2018, 121–124.

Peters, Ronald, Regina Jones Johnson, Charles Savage, Angela Meshack, Paula Espinoza, and Troy Jefferson. "Female and Relationship Devaluation among African American and Latino American Youth: Is What's Normal Really Normal?" *Journal of Child & Adolescent Trauma* 3, no. 1 (2010): 13–24.

Petrosky, Emiko, Janet M. Blair, Carter J. Betz, Katherine A. Fowler, Shane PD Jack, and Bridget H. Lyons. "Racial and Ethnic Differences in Homicides of Adult Women and the Role of Intimate Partner Violence—United States, 2003–2014." *MMWR. Morbidity and Mortality Weekly Report* 66, no. 28 (2017): 741.

Pierre, Martin R., Malcolm H. Woodland, and James R. Mahalik. "The Effects of Racism, African Self-consciousness and Psychological Functioning on Black Masculinity: A Historical and Social Adaptation Framework." *Journal of African American Men* 6, no. 2 (2001): 19–39.

Pinn, Anthony B. "'Gettin'grown': Notes on Gangsta Rap Music and Notions of Manhood." *Journal of African American Men* 1, no. 4 (1996): 23–35.

Poniewozik, James. 2016. "In FX's 'Atlanta,' a Princeton Dropout Works the Angles Back Home." *The New York Times*, September 6, 2016. https://www.nytimes.com /2016/09/06/arts/television/atlanta-fx-donald-glover.html

Randolph, Antonia. "When Men Give Birth to Intimacy: The Case of Jay-Z's '4: 44.'" *Journal of African American Studies* 22, no. 4 (2018): 393–406.

Randolph, Robert. "Moonlight, Barry Jenkins." *Queer Studies in Media & Popular-Culture, 2, no 3* (2017): 383–387.

Reeves, Mosi. 2017. "Jay-Z Is Vulnerable, Apologetic and Still Dazzling on '4:44.'" *Rolling Stone*, July 5, 2017. https://www.rollingstone.com/music/music

-album-reviews/review-jay-z-is-vulnerable-apologetic-and-still-dazzling-on
-444-123022/

Rich, John A., and Courtney M. Grey. "Pathways to Recurrent Trauma among Young Black Men: Traumatic Stress, Substance Use, and the "Code of the Street." *American Journal of Public Health* 95, no. 5 (2005): 816–824.

Rinelli, Lauren N., and Susan L. Brown. "Race Differences in Union Transitions among Cohabitors: The Role of Relationship Features." *Marriage & Family Review* 46, no. 1–2 (2010): 22–40.

Roberson, Patricia N. E., Jerika C. Norona, Katherine A. Lenger, and Spencer B. Olmstead. "How do Relationship Stability and Quality Affect Wellbeing?: Romantic Relationship Trajectories, Depressive Symptoms, and Life Satisfaction across 30 years." *Journal of Child and Family Studies* 27, no. 7 (2018): 2171–2184.

Rodriguez, Rene. 2016. "Miami plays a starring role in the glorious 'Moonlight.'" *Miami Herald,* October 21, 2016. https://www.miamiherald.com/entertainment/movies-news-reviews/article109699627.html

Roy, Kevin M., and Omari Dyson. "Making Daddies into Fathers: Community-based Fatherhood Programs and the Construction of Masculinities for Low-income African American Men." *American Journal of Community Psychology* 45, no. 1–2 (2010): 139–154.

Sassler, Sharon, Katherine Michelmore, and Zhenchao Qian. "Transitions from Sexual Relationships into Cohabitation and Beyond." *Demography* 55, no. 2 (2018): 511–534.

Seaton, Gregory. "Toward a Theoretical Understanding of Hypermasculine Coping among Urban Black Adolescent Males." *Journal of Human Behavior in the Social Environment* 15, no. 2–3 (2007): 367–390.

Sheffield, Rob. 2018. "'Atlanta' is Simply the Best Show on TV." *Rolling Stone,* March 8, 2018. https://www.rollingstone.com/tv/tv-reviews/atlanta-is-simply-the-best-show-on-tv-127644/

Shelton-Wheeler, Feliesha. "African American Male-Female Romantic Relationships." In *Love, Intimacy, and the African American Couple,* edited by Katherine M. Helm and Jon Carlson, New York: Routledge. 2013, 63–84.

Simons, Ronald L., Leslie G. Simons, Man K. Lei, and Antoinette M. Landor. "Relational Schemas, Hostile Romantic Relationships, and Beliefs about Marriage among Young African American Adults." *Journal of Social and Personal Relationships* 29, no. 1 (2012): 77–101.

Sitgraves, Claudia. "The Benefits of Marriage for African American Men." *Research Brief* 10 (2008).

Slatton, Brittany C., and Kamesha Spates. *Hyper Sexual, Hyper Masculine?: Gender, Race and Sexuality in the Identities of Contemporary Black Men.* New York: Routledge, 2016.

Staggers-Hakim, Raja. "The Nation's Unprotected Children and the Ghost of Mike Brown, or the Impact of National Police Killings on the Health and Social Development of African American Boys." *Journal of Human Behavior in the Social Environment* 26, no. 3–4 (2016): 390–399.

Steele, Fiona, Constantinos Kallis, Harvey Goldstein, and Heather Joshi. "The Relationship between Childbearing and Transitions from Marriage and Cohabitation in Britain." *Demography* 42, no. 4 (2005): 647–673.

Sullivan, Jas, and Ashraf, E. M. *African American Identity: Racial and cultural dimensions of the Black experience.* Lanham, MD: Lexington Books, 2012.

U.S. Census Bureau. "Median Income in the past 12 months. 2017 American Community Survey 1-Year Estimates." Washington, DC: Author. 2017.

Vespa, Jonathan. "Relationship Transitions among Older Cohabitors: The Role of Health, Wealth, and Family Ties." *Journal of Marriage and Family* 75, no. 4 (2013): 933–949.

Wallace, Riley. (2017). "Where Does Kendrick Lamar's 'DUCKWORTH.' Rank Among Best Hip Hop Stories?" *HipHopDx,* April 15, 2017. https://hiphopdx.com /editorials/id.3729/title.where-does-kendrick-lamars-duckworth-rank-among-best -hip-hop-stories#

Wanzo, Rebecca. "Black love is not a fairytale." *Poroi* 7, no. 2 (2011): 5.

Watters, John K., and Patrick Biernacki. "Targeted Sampling: Options for the Study of Hidden Populations." *Social Problems* 36, no. 4 (1989): 416–430.

Welch, Tim, Erica Rouleau-Mitchell, Adam Farero, E. Megan Lachmar, and Andrea K. Wittenborn. "Maintaining Relationship Quality During the Transition to Parenthood: The Need for Next Generation Interventions." *Contemporary Family Therapy* 41, no. 2 (2019): 211–218.

West, Carolyn M. "'A Thin Line Between Love and Hate'? Black Men as Victims and Perpetrators of Dating Violence." *Journal of Aggression, Maltreatment & Trauma* 16, no. 3 (2008): 238–257.

Whiteneir Jr, Kevin Talmer. "Dig if you will the Picture: Prince's Subversion of Hegemonic Black Masculinity, and the Fallacy of Racial Transcendence." *Howard Journal of Communications* 30, no. 2 (2019): 129–143.

# Index

131; from infidelity, 84–85, 131; intimate partner/domestic violence and, 76, 81, 83–84, 131; with law enforcement and criminal justice system interactions, 75–76; with miscarriages, 80–81; physical abuse, 81–84; police officer exposure to, 78–80; prior research lacking on black men/boys, 5, 73, 75–76; psychological, 76, 77–81, 130–31; relationship trajectories impacted by, 4, 5, *25*, 53, 73, 75–91, 102–3, 124, 131; as relationship transition factor, 102–3; research deficit on black men/boys impacts from, 5, 73, 76–77; risky behavior and disease relation to childhood, 73; from sexual abuse in childhood, 82–83, 85, 92, 131; from slavery, contemporary impacts of, 73–74, 77–78, 91, 131; substance abuse relation to, 75, 77; trust impacted by, 89–91, 92, 102–3, 131; women's aggressive and abusive behavior role in, 76, 81–82, 85

*Treme*, 7

trust/trustworthiness, *25*; as commitment factor, 100, 132; divorce impacting future, 92, 96, 99; divorce rooted in lack of, 90–91; as ideal partner trait, *37, 47, 49*; infidelity impacting, 63–64, 110; marriage impacted by issues of, 90–91, 102–3, 111, 132; racism influence on relationship, 15; separations in marriage and, 102–3, 111; social networking impacting, 16; trauma impact on, 89–91, 92, 102–3, 131; women's ex-partners and issues of, 89–90

*Two Centuries of Black Louisville* (Aubespin and Hudson), 28–29

union/unity, 1, 13, 17, *37, 45, 47*, 107

vulnerability, expressions of, 2, 4, 11–12, 131

*When the Bough Breaks*, 8
*Why Did I Get Married Too?*, 7
women: aggressive and abusive behavior from, 76, 81–82, 85; cohabitation for, studies on, 93–94; confidence of, views on, *35, 39, 41, 43, 45, 47, 49, 51*; economic motivations in marriage for, 13; emotional attachment for, with casual sex, 59–60, 61, 71, 130; ex-partners of, trust issues around, 89–90; independence of, impacts of, 17; infidelity by, 63–64, 84–85; infidelity temptations from, 64–65; intimacy for, 69–71; intimate partner violence by and towards, 76; marriage pressures from, 101; marriage separation initiated by, 104–5, 111; participant advice for, on partner selection, 135–36; participants on ideal traits for, *23, 35, 37, 39, 41, 43, 45, 47, 49, 51*, 53, 98–99, 100, 117; relationship transitions for, studies on, 93–94; role models treatment of, impact of, 78, 117–18, 143; sex and commitment pressures from, 59; sexuality impacted by relationship transitions of, 94; sexual objectification of, media role in, 67–68; sexual promiscuity of, views on, 56, 60; sexual stereotypes about black, 56, 138

# About the Authors

**Armon R. Perry**, PhD, MSW, is a professor at the University of Louisville's Kent School of Social Work. Dr. Perry's research interests include fathers' involvement in the lives of their children and African American men's contributions to family functioning. Currently, Dr. Perry serves as the principal investigator of the 4 Your Child Program, a federally funded multi-site project that aims to increase non-custodial fathers' capacity for paternal involvement. In addition to his teaching and research, Dr. Perry has professional experience in the areas of child protective services and as a parent education curriculum facilitator.

**Siobhan Smith-Jones**, PhD, is associate professor in the Department of Communication at the University of Louisville. She is also a proud graduate of Xavier University of Louisiana and Louisiana State University. Her current research interests include explorations of African American women as interpretive communities. She teaches courses in mass media, race, culture, fandom, and media literacy. She co-authored a special edition of *Women & Language* with Dr. Karla Scott and Dr. Cerise Glenn, which focused on FLOTUS Michelle Obama. She was co-investigator on a $397,000 National Institutes of Health grant with Dr. Lindsay Della, Dr. Margaret D'Silva, and other professors at the University of Louisville. She has served on the Board of the Organization for the Study of Communication, Language, and Gender, and as Secretary and Chair of the Nominating Committee of the Mass Communication Division of the National Communication Association. She is past president of the Kentucky Communication Association and received the OSCLG Feminist Mentor Teacher of the Year Award in 2017.

**Cheri Langley**, PhD, MPH, CHES, is a program manager at the University of Louisville's Kent School of Social Work. In the last seven years, Dr. Langley has managed two separate federally funded grant projects totaling $10 million in the areas of teenage pregnancy prevention and responsible fatherhood respectively. In addition to her experience in managing large funded projects and conducting research on adolescent sexual health, Dr. Langley also has national and international experience as a certified Community Health Educator working with low income youth and adult populations.

**Azaliah Israel**, PhD, is currently a postdoctoral scholar at Penn State University and a policy associate with the Research-to-Policy Collaboration (RPC). In December 2019, Dr. Israel earned her PhD at the University of Arkansas in the public policy program with a specialization in family policy. Her dissertation "The Social Construction of Black Fatherhood in Responsible Fatherhood Policies" is being prepared for journal submission. She specializes in advocating for black fathers in the areas of research, policy, and capacity building for non-profit fatherhood organizations.

www.ingramcontent.com/pod-product-compliance
Lightning Source LLC
Chambersburg PA
CBHW022320280326
41932CB00010B/1168